What Others are Saying About
God of Hope

"God's story is the big story in this book and the reason for hope. With gripping transparency the author tells his own story of struggling with and trusting in the God of hope. The genuine openness with which that struggle is told draws the reader and makes the author's account of deepening trust in God intriguing. Dave Illingworth's story invites the reader to turn from despair and loss of hope to God's story of hope through His Son. The book's story of human struggle and faith makes placing trust in God all the more inviting to the reader."

Dr. Ronald Manahan, *president*
Grace College & Theological Seminary, Winona Lake, Ind.

"I think it's fantastic that Dave has chosen to share his story as well as use his creative talents to encourage and inspire others in their spiritual walk. I'm sure *God of Hope* will impact many."

Joe Gibbs, *Pro Football Hall of Fame head coach and owner of Joe Gibbs Racing*

"The first time I met Dave I knew there was something special about him. He is a very sincere man and I could tell he loves the Lord. This project is so Dave--it covers all the bases and pays close attention to detail. I love the way it connects my story, His story and your story. *God of Hope* will reach many souls and make a huge difference in believers' and non-believers' lives. I've been involved in many Christian projects: this is the best one yet!

Darrell Waltrip, *NASCAR champion, Hall of Fame nominee and Fox broadcaster*

God of Hope is a compelling series of stories that bear witness to the presence and power of God, who is our hope. Dave Illingworth is a marvelous storyteller, who brings to life the personality, experience, and faith of four central biblical figures: Thomas, Moses, Paul, and John. Dave's gripping prose is grounded on solid scholarship. Thus, his creative retelling of the biblical story is historically accurate as well as theologically faithful. Using the strands of his own testimony as well as biblical truth, Dave weaves a tapestry that celebrates God's grand narrative for history, urging us to participate in this story as people of hope. *God of Hope* will encourage believers even as it invites all people to join in the drama of God's redeeming love.

Dr. Mark D. Roberts, *Senior Director and Scholar-in-Residence for Laity Lodge, Kerrville, Texas*

GOD OF HOPE

GOD OF HOPE

**FOUR MEN ENTER OUR WORLD
WITH THE PLAN
GENESIS THROUGH REVELATION**

J.DAVIS ILLINGWORTH, JR.

BMH Books
www.bmhbooks.com
Winona Lake, IN 46590

God of Hope
Four Men Enter Our World with the Plan
Genesis through Revelation

Copyright © J. Davis Illingworth, Jr. 2010

ISBN: 978-0-88469-271-3
RELIGION / Christian Theology / Apologetics

Published by BMH books, Winona Lake, IN 46590
www.bmhbooks.com

Printed in the United States of America

Dedication

*For my wife Cynthia
who stayed at home and raised five children
while I went out and played.*

Table of Contents

Introduction

I hesitate to tell my story and write about God's plan for my life. I hesitate because I have lived in Irvine, California, for most of the last twenty-eight years. It is a model community where everyone has a swimming pool, the sun always shines, and there are no cemeteries. I am seemingly healthy, unscarred, and untested. Why would anyone be interested in my story?

I hesitate to tell God's story and write about His plan for humanity. I hesitate because I am not an ordained minister and have no formal training in theology. My only qualification is that I was once a third grade Sunday school teacher. Why would anyone listen to me?

I hesitate to write about your story and God's plan for your life. I hesitate because people who profess to have all the answers to questions about God that can't be answered should not be trusted. Why should anyone trust me?

Despite my hesitation, I am telling my story because, regardless of the outward appearance of health and success, I am the same hurt and insecure boy of my childhood. The years have covered over and buried all the pain and disappointment. We're all hiding behind veiled faces, not wanting each other to know who we really are or what problems we have. I am no different, carrying my burdens inside, wearing the mask of everyday politeness while bravely holding on.

Despite my hesitation, I am writing about God's story, but you will notice that what I have written is heavily footnoted because I have relied on the Bible and the writing of serious theologians. It is my prayer that what I have written will harm no one and help some.

And, despite my hesitation, I am writing about your story. I don't have the answers to many of your questions because there are things I don't understand and don't know. What I do know is not so much an answer as a hope, the God of Hope who has overcome death.

J. Davis Illingworth, Jr.

Part I

MY STORY:
GOD'S PLAN FOR MY LIFE

Chapter 1

Playing Chess with God

I grew up in Wheeling, West Virginia, where my father was a minister at Vance Memorial Presbyterian Church. Growing up a preacher's kid was full of challenges. The congregation acted as the conduct police—rules, rules, rules—always watching for misbehavior. I thought of God as a distant, unfeeling, unfair drill sergeant. I was a borderline believer, trying to please my parents. I kept God at a safe distance, and unless there was a problem, I didn't bother Him so that He wouldn't bother me.

When I went to college, I drifted into non-belief, and for the first time I came in contact with atheists. They seemed like brave, intelligent people who were challenging the great majority and were masters of their universe. How could any intelligent person believe this rubbish about a God? It was all a myth.

At Christmas time 1974, we were visiting my wife Cynthia's family in Chinook, Montana, and I had babysitter duty. Our five-month-old son Spencer was taking his afternoon nap. Since his birth, I had been asking questions and seeking answers. *Who am I? Where am I? What am I doing here?* Far away voices had been pulling at me for some time. I didn't want to believe; I wanted to disbelieve, but my deeper instinct could not stop believing. I sat down in a comfortable chair in front of the fireplace and casually picked up a Bible lying nearby. I opened it to the Gospel of Mark and read it from beginning to end. When I finished, I realized that my life was changed, and I had to make a decision. This was not about my wife, my son, or my parents; it was about me. How was *I* going to respond to God?

That afternoon I met a different God, and I was stunned. How could I have been so wrong? How could I have missed this? This was a God I wanted to know and could follow—an intimate, direct-dealing, un-controlling, and forgiving God, who asked for my free obedience. It was a defining moment in my life. At that moment I believed in my heart and asked Jesus Christ into my life.

At the time I was a staff manager in the Portland, Oregon, region of Chrysler Corporation. Cynthia and I had been married three years and had moved three times. In 1976 I was promoted to assistant regional manager for the San Francisco region, and we moved a fourth time in five years.

We enjoyed San Francisco, loved our home, joined a great church, and had wonderful friends. We were blessed with two more sons, Trevor and Blair. For the first time, we were putting down roots, and I dreaded the thought of moving again. We began giving 10 percent of our income to the church, and I started looking for a job in a retail dealership so we would not have to move again.

In 1978 the economy was struggling and Chrysler was having serious financial problems—forecasting losses of more than six hundred million dollars. At the end of each quarter John Riccardo, the CEO of Chrysler, would come to San Francisco to call on the presidents of the Bank of America, Wells Fargo, and Crocker Bank to secure lines of credit. He was a humble, honest man who travelled alone. On three different occasions I was assigned to drive him to his meetings. At the end of the year, Mr. Riccardo approached the U.S. Government, asking for loan guarantees to secure the lines of credit, but his request met with some opposition. The decisions Mr. Riccardo was about to make would affect the direction of my life.

In early 1979 I was promoted to be the Cleveland regional manager. At 35 I would be the youngest regional manager in the company. The region covered all of northern Ohio and western Pennsylvania. It was a huge opportunity, but I was badly shaken. I did not want to move cross-country with three young sons. Exchanging San Francisco for Cleveland in 1979 was not very attractive.

Upset, confused, and angry, I got in my car, drove out of town, and parked under the San Mateo Bridge. I pleaded with God that we not have to move to Cleveland. I negotiated with God. I bargained that if we didn't sell the house before I left for Cleveland, I would take it as a sign from God that we were to stay in San Francisco and I was to go into retail. It was Tuesday.

I called my assistant to make flight reservations to Cleveland, expecting to leave the next day. United Airlines was on strike, and the first flight I could get was a red-eye on Sunday night on American Airlines.

I called a real estate agent and set the selling price on our home on the high side. The agent was not optimistic. It would take a week or more to list the house, and at the price I was asking, it was going to take a while, which was okay with me.

My father had always told me that God has a purpose and a plan for the lives of those who love Him (Romans 8:28). My father said that if he would play a game of chess with a master chess player like Bobby Fischer, no matter what move he would make on the board, Bobby Fischer would win. Similarly, in the game of life, God will always win but in a positive way. No matter what decision we make in life, God will make His move on the board of life that will get us who love Him where we are supposed to be when we are supposed to be there to fulfill His purpose and plan for our lives.

Our house had not even been listed yet, when two prospective buyers viewed the house on Saturday morning. The first couple offered us full price, and the second couple offered more than the asking price. Checkmate! We were moving to Cleveland, Ohio.

Chapter 2
Lost in Detroit

The Chrysler financial crisis deepened and Volkswagen made an offer to buy the company. The U.S. government did not want a German company to have access to the M60 tanks built by Chrysler for the Army and agreed to the loan guarantees. However, there were two conditions: The M-60 tank division had to be sold off and John Riccardo had to resign. Lee Iacocca from Ford took over the leadership of Chrysler.

The Chrysler field regional managers from across the country were called to the headquarters in Detroit for several days of meetings. All the department heads, advertising, distribution, market representation, etc. stood before us for two days, lecturing about what we were doing wrong and what we and the dealers needed to do to bring Chrysler back to profitability. It was a one-way conversation. Headquarters was in complete control. On the morning of the third day we were to have a meeting with Lee Iacocca in the Green Room of the KT Keller building.

Iacocca strode into the room, chomping on a cigar. For thirty minutes he cursed and raged on about the banks, the government, and the dealers, attacking everyone about everything. It was a blistering attack, and finally, he got around to us. "If you can't get the job done," he ranted, "let me know because there are plenty of people at Ford who can!" He got a standing ovation, and I stood and applauded with the others. But as I applauded, I had an overwhelming sensation from deep inside that I was not where I was supposed to be.

The first week in August of 1979 Cynthia and the boys arrived from California, and we moved into our home in Cleveland. The very next week the Cleveland region was closed, and I was demoted and transferred to the Detroit regional office. Angry and frustrated, I contacted an executive search firm and sent out three hundred résumés.

I had just completed an advertising meeting with the Dodge dealers in Grand Rapids, Michigan, on a cold, gloomy day in early November. It was late afternoon and as I glanced at the clock on the dash, I noted that I should have plenty of time to get back to the Birmingham Sheraton, where I was staying, by eight o'clock.

Cynthia was at home with three small boys, ages five, three, and two. We had been separated almost the entire year, and the strain on our marriage was beginning to show. One small act had helped: Every night at exactly eight o'clock I called home.

On that dark November night as I approached Detroit, it was raining and trying to snow. Suddenly, I realized I was no longer on Route 96 but was on Route 696. Where was I? What happened? Panic started to settle in. Everything was unfamiliar and the signs were hard to read. I spotted an exit, Telegraph Road, and pulled off. Traffic was at an absolute standstill. The clock read 7:10 p.m.

My head started to pound. Gritting my teeth, I yanked back hard on the steering wheel. "Come on-n-n, Lord!" I muttered. "After the year I've had, the least You can do is get me back to the hotel by eight!"

I turned the radio on, but the constant gibberish annoyed me so I turned it off. The incessant thumping of the windshield wipers annoyed me even more.

"Are You aware that they closed the Cleveland region?" I asked sarcastically. "I've started giving 10 percent to the church, and what happens? I get transferred, demoted, and transferred again. The company could go into bankruptcy; I can't sell my home in Cleveland that I have owned for just one week. Look what my family has to endure. Are You even there? Do You care?" I shouted out loud.

Exasperated, I leaned forward on the steering wheel, trying to read signs. I turned right on Thirteen Mile Road and inched my way to Woodward Avenue. It was 7:30 p.m. Should I stop at a pay phone? No, the traffic was better, so I pressed hard on the gas, racing in and out of traffic. "Why don't You do something, Lord?" I shouted. "You're doing nothing! Nothing!" I hissed angrily.

I looked for familiar surroundings but realized I was lost. "All right!" I yelled. "Just get me back to the hotel by eight! I know I have to turn right, but where? SHOW ME WHERE TO TURN RIGHT!" Several streets flashed by, and unexpectedly I made a hard right turn down a dimly lit residential street, Wimbilton. The further I drove, the more alarmed I became. The street came to an intersection. "THIS CAN'T BE RIGHT!" I shouted out. Frustrated, I turned hard to the right, spinning the wheels of my Dodge Charger in wet leaves—more houses, more streets. I turned left. Another long, winding residential street, Dorchester. Huge trees straddled both sides of the street, making it appear like an endless dark tunnel. It was 7:45 p.m.

I slowed down as a sense of betrayal swept through me. I would never get to the hotel by eight. It was hopeless. I snapped! I stood on the brakes hard and the car slid sideways, bouncing off the curb. I got out of the car and slammed the door with all my might. I kicked at the car, shaking my fist at the sky and cursing God. "ANSWER ME"! I demanded of God. "ARE YOU THERE?" I stormed around the car, kicking the tires, raging at God. "YOU'RE USELESS! NO GOOD! WHERE ARE YOU? WHAT ARE YOU DOING? I'M DOING MY PART. YOU'RE NOT DOING YOURS"! I vented all my anger and frustration until I was exhausted.

Then, wearily I climbed back into the car and looked in the rearview mirror. I was a pitiful sight. The building dam of pressure over the last year was ready to burst. I was hurt and afraid—hurt by what I felt was betrayal but more afraid than anything. Afraid that I believed in a God who wasn't there or, worse yet, didn't care. I brushed away the tears that began to well up in my eyes. There was no need to cry but soon I was, with great choking sobs. Then it became strangely quiet as if nothing was ever going to happen again. I suddenly felt that there was hope. It was a defining moment. I just had to believe and place my hope and trust in an invisible God who cares. It was 7:55 p.m. I resigned myself to the fact that, if I didn't get back to the hotel by eight, it would be okay.

I started up the car and began to slowly drive down to the end of the street. It emptied into a large lighted parking lot that was part of a shopping mall. In front of me was a loading dock with a large sign that read, "Delivery Trucks Only." I was at the service entrance of the Birmingham Sheraton.

Chapter 3

Home at Last

We sold our home in Cleveland. I rented a home in Detroit for six months because I believed I was going to change jobs. I sent out three hundred more résumés, but the country was in an economic recession, and I had not one response.

Ed Fitzpatrick and I had roomed together as trainees back when I started at Chrysler. He now worked for a small Japanese company, Toyota, in Los Angeles and arranged an interview for me. Toyota was interested in me, but they had no openings.

It was now February, and I was worried. I had been actively looking for a new job since August and had had only one interview. Nothing was happening. One morning on the way to work about 6:30 a.m., I pulled into the parking lot of the Birmingham airport. It was bitter cold outside with a light snow on the ground. I let the car idle.

I sat there and asked God if He really wanted me to leave Chrysler. Was that overwhelming sensation to leave real, or was I mistaken? If I was to leave I needed some reassurance.

I pulled out the small New Testament Bible from the inside of my left coat pocket, opened it and laid it on my lap. "This is crazy" I thought to myself. Then I placed my right index finger on a page and I looked down. My finger was resting on John 14:1, "Do not worry or be upset but believe in God, believe also in me".

But I was worried and upset. I had signed a six-month lease and needed to buy a house in Detroit or move by June 30. Shouldn't there be a time schedule? If I don't have a new job by such and such a date, is it a sign I am to stay with Chrysler? How about sixty days; if I don't have a new job in sixty days, I stay with Chrysler.

When I got to my office, I pulled out a calendar and counted off sixty days. It didn't make sense. It would be Sunday, April 6. Why would anyone offer me a job on a Sunday or weekend? I circled Friday, April 4. If I didn't have a new job by then, it would be a sign that I was to buy a home in Detroit and stay with Chrysler.

I mailed out more résumés but still heard nothing back. The second week in March my boss, the Detroit regional manager, Frank Hoag, called me into his office. He knew I was not happy and that I was looking for another job. Chrysler wanted me to stay. He told me the two of us were to meet with his boss, the central area manager, Hank Savoy, and that I was going to be offered a tremendous opportunity. I was considered high potential. Mr. Iacocca was concerned that, with all the people moving into the company from Ford, Chrysler people would feel they did not have a chance for advancement. He wanted to showcase a Chrysler manager and I was being considered to be his assistant.

I staggered back to my office. *What am I to do, Lord? Does this mean I am to stay?* As I began to waver, I was again filled with that overwhelming sensation from deep inside that I was not where I was supposed to be.

Frank and I went to meet Hank Savoy. I turned down the job, but they kept talking and talking and talking, and it became clear that this was a job I would not be allowed to refuse. What was I supposed to do? Suddenly, I blurted out, "I have three priorities in my life: #1 is Jesus Christ; #2 is my family; and #3 is Chrysler. I believe if I take this job, it will be changing my #1 and #2 priorities, and I just can't do that."

In my mind I am screaming at myself, *"Are you crazy? What's wrong with you? You're throwing away your career!"*

A heavy silence hung in the air. Hank slapped his hands together and said, "Well, that's it. This meeting is over."

The weeks passed in silence. Every day I died a little bit more and clung to John 14:1. I called Toyota to follow up, but they still had nothing. After eight months and more than six hundred résumés, Toyota was the only interview I had.

At five o'clock on April 4, 1980, I stood looking out my office window, confused and uncertain but not doubting. That overwhelming sensation must have been wrong. Whatever God's plan or purpose was, I would accept it. Cynthia and I would get a real estate agent and start looking for a home in Detroit that weekend. I would stay at Chrysler.

Saturday morning, April 5, 1980, I was sitting at the kitchen table, drinking a cup of coffee. It had been fifty-nine days. The phone rang. It was Jim Press from Toyota. It had been a hectic week because of the Toyota Grand Prix at Long Beach. He apologized. He had been unable to call me earlier in the week but wanted to offer me the job as assistant to the national sales manager for Toyota.

One month later I was working at Toyota. My second day on the job, I attended the monthly president's sales meeting. All the field regional managers from across the country came to headquarters once a month for this meeting. The president, Mr. Makino, opened the meeting with a short welcoming statement. Then he sat down. All the Toyota regional managers from around the country sat around a U-shaped table and looked out on the national department heads: advertising, distribution, market representation, etc. Each regional manager addressed headquarters, reporting about what was happening in his local market. What the service and product issues were that needed to be addressed. What the competition was doing. What the dealers needed to do to be more competitive. The headquarters department heads listened to what the field managers had to say, and there was a vigorous two-way discussion.

As I settled in and listened, I was filled with an overwhelming sense from deep inside that I was finally where I was supposed to be, home at last.

Chapter 4

An Answer to Prayer?

That was thirty years ago. During the subsequent years, Cynthia and I were blessed with two more children, a son Greer and a daughter Emily. I had more than twenty different jobs with Toyota. I helped start up the Lexus Division, and I was named "Automobile Man of the Year" for my efforts. While running the Toyota Division, I was named "Top Newsmaker" by *Automotive News* for my efforts in establishing the Toyota Camry as the number one selling car in America. Near the end of my career, I was named senior vice president and chief planning and administrative officer of Toyota Motor Sales, USA, Inc. I was responsible for corporate planning, advanced product planning, product planning, corporate services, finance, information systems, human resources, legal, University of Toyota, and Motorsports (Indy cars, NASCAR).

In 1980 when I started at Toyota, I began to write short stories. In my prayer life, at the end of every prayer, I asked God if someday I could be an author and speaker pleasing to Him. I wrote "Cain's Predicament" about a Vietnam veteran, but no one would publish it. In 1982 I submitted a short story to *Guidepost Magazine,* but it was rejected. In 1986 I submitted "Lost in Detroit" to *Guidepost* and it was rejected. In the late 1980s I wrote a manuscript entitled "Lies, Lies, Lies." I contacted publishers like Thomas Nelson, Crossway, and Zondervan, but all rejected my proposal. In 1994 I wrote a manuscript about the start of Lexus, "Lexus Right from the Start," but could not find an agent willing to take it. In 1996 I met with a publisher in New York on the Lexus story but was again rejected.

While the head of the Lexus and Toyota Divisions, I had success in writing and delivering short motivational speeches for dealer meetings. Speeches about such diverse subjects as the conquering of Mt. Everest, Abraham Lincoln, man's first trip to the moon, Walt Disney, Vince Lombardi, and Bill Walsh. I estimate that over the next twenty years, from 1980 to 2000, I had asked God more than six thousand times to be an author and speaker pleasing to Him. Having had little success, I decided His answer was a quiet, "No thank you," and I stopped asking.

In the summer of 2005 I started participating in a Wednesday morning thirty-minute national conference call for an organization called Impact XXI. Each week a guest speaker talked about how business leaders can make a difference in the world. One morning the speaker was Chip Ingram of Living on the Edge.org. He remarked that he had noticed many baby boomers were reaching the end of their business careers and were being reminded by God of promises they had made when they were younger to do something for Him. Chip Ingram's words took me back more than fifty years to my childhood in West Virginia.

When I was growing up in Wheeling, my father always gave a fictional first person account of the Nativity on Christmas Eve. One year he would be a shepherd, the next year the innkeeper, the year after that a wise man. I found these sermons vague and unsatisfying because they were not about the main characters and lacked detail and emotion, but the congregation loved them. As I listened to those sermons, I silently promised God, "Someday, I will write about the encounter between the unbelieving Thomas and Jesus, and I will do it right."

I tried to push aside Chip Ingram's comments and forget about my childhood commitment. After all, I am a careful, controlled, successful business executive. This was crazy, but uneasiness continued to stir inside me. Several months later I was driving on a Los Angeles freeway and noticed a sign by the road that read, "City of Los Angeles—population 3,772,000." My childhood promise came to mind. Certainly the people of L.A. needed to hear the gospel. I started to pray, but who was I to do something like that? There are over three million people in Los Angeles. Certainly there is someone more qualified than I. I have a big job, a wife and five children to take care of. I'm too busy! Who would listen to me? Besides, I stopped writing. *I thought You told me "No thank you." Why now? Why me?*

The answer did not come in a brilliant flash of light or a loud audible voice like a thundering waterfall but from inner words spoken deep inside, "Because you can!" It was another significant moment. I changed my focus from selling cars to selling God.

But this would be different from cars. There would be no business plan. Success would not be measured by profits, sales, or number of conversions. The approach would need to be different, creative, authentic, opening up new possibilities for people to hear about God. This would not be about selling anything, but it would be about opening hearts and minds to the opportunity of a relationship with the God of the universe.

What I thought was going to take a couple of months has turned into a more than four-year struggle. I have found myself always praying, thinking, reading and writing—on airplanes, in hotel rooms, driving the car, at four o'clock in the morning. Today, I have more questions about God than when I started. Some very personal questions, some very angry but honest questions. I also discovered things about God, myself, the universe, and those around me that I could never have imagined. Do I choose to accept the lie that I am nothing but a talking animal whose existence is pointless, living without hope, ending in death? Or, do I choose to believe the truth that I am made in the image of God and that my existence has purpose, living with hope, ending in life?

That's my story, but what about God's story? I ask you to listen to four men who will tell you about God's plan for humanity that has been unfolding for thousands of years. They will tell you about how He is going to rid the universe of evil and heal and restore His creation from the damage that has been done. They will also suggest the part you can choose to play in God's unfolding story.

Part II

HIS STORY:
GOD'S PLAN FOR HUMANITY

Chapter 5

The Disciple Thomas
Listen to Your Heart

Pastor:
This morning
something unusual happened.
Four strangers came to my office.
They have asked to speak to you.
Who they are,
where they are from,
and what they have to say
I will leave to them
to explain.
Before he begins
each has asked that someone read Scripture.

Now Thomas…one of the twelve, was not with the disciples when Jesus came. So the other disciples told him, "We have seen the Lord!"
But he said to them, "Unless I see the nail marks in his hands and put my fingers where the nails were, and put my hand into his side, I will not believe it."
A week later his disciples were in the house again, and Thomas was with them. Though the doors were locked, Jesus came and stood among them and said, "Peace be with you!" Then he said to Thomas, "Put your fingers here; see my hands. Reach out your hand and put it into my side. Stop doubting and believe."
Thomas said to him, "My Lord and my God!" (John 20:24-28 NIV)

My name is Thomas.
The God of Abraham and Moses,
the one true God of the universe,
has granted me this opportunity
to step across space and time,
from His space,
the Kingdom of Heaven,
into your space
Earth,
so I can tell you my story.
God wants me
to share my story with you
so you will know
how wide and long and high and deep[1]
is the love
of God and His Son,
for His creation,
for Earth,
and His love for you.

Before I begin,
please stand that we may join together in prayer.

"Take Away My Doubt"

God on High,
Hear this prayer.
Are you there?
Are you real?
Do you care how I feel?

The world is wrong.
Death and suffering are all around.
Lord, take away my doubt.
Why don't you show Yourself to me?

I'm too busy,
Far too much to do.
Why should I slow down?
And tell me why I should believe
In someone who hides from me like You.

Am I lost and can't be found?
Blind and cannot see?
Jesus, take away the doubt from me.

Amen

Two-thousand years ago
I was one of the twelve disciples
of the Messiah,
Jesus of Nazareth.
Jerusalem,
a city of almost seventy-five thousand,[2]
was the center of culture and commerce for the Middle East.
The Roman Emperor, Tiberius,
had appointed Pontius Pilate,
a corrupt and violent man,
Governor of Judea.[3]
I lived in Galilee
about eighty miles north of Jerusalem.[4]
Herod Antipas
had been given authority over Galilee.
He ruled with casual savagery.
It was Antipas
who, after being aroused
by a teenage dancer,
granted her wish
that John the Baptist,
a righteous and innocent man,
be executed,
his head cut off

and presented to her on a platter.[5]
Under Roman rule,
the earth was filled with greed and smeared with blood.
Rome had no fear of God.

Israel's religious leaders,
the scribes and Pharisees,
held offices of influence under Pilate and Herod.
They intimidated and controlled us with countless rules,
always blaming,
always accusing,
always disagreeing with each other.
The basic dignity and genuine needs of the people,
the people they had been called to shepherd,
were ignored.[6]

Without a shepherd,
I found that my own mind had become twisted.
I believed that the only way we,
the chosen people of God,
could earn His blessing
was through
grim obedience to
the law given to us by Moses
and taught by the scribes.

But my heart
was filled with hatred for the Romans,
bitterness toward Herod,
and I feared the scribes and Pharisees.
It seemed as though
God had turned His face away from Israel forever.
Then,
after four-hundred years of silence,
God spoke through a man,
John the Baptist,

who appeared in the wilderness and began to stir
expectations—
mine and my people's.[7]
It was being whispered
that God was again acting in the world.
The long-awaited Messiah was coming.
He would restore Israel
and free us
from the evil that was Rome.
He would set all creation right again.
All that had been lost when
Adam and Eve turned away from God
would be restored.

Not long after,
a new prophet,
Jesus of Nazareth,
came to my village.
A young man
of great strength and courage,
He spoke in measured and deliberate tones,
taught with great authority,
and had a deep magic.
His message was liberating and empowering.
His rules were not about what I should not do,
but about what I should do:[8]
Love God and love my neighbor.[9]

I instinctively liked Him.
I was drawn to Him
and was chosen
as one of His twelve disciples.
I was with Jesus
continually
for about two years.[10]
Everywhere we went

hope and excitement followed.[11]
People were always crowding around Him,
pushing,
shoving,
pleading for His attention.
In the evening,
away from the crowds,
we all told stories and laughed by the fire.
His laugh,
always made me smile.
When I went to sleep at night,
Jesus would still be up.
When I got up in the morning,
He would already be awake.

During those two years
there were a
few occasions,
not many,
when we were alone together.
He put His hand on my shoulder
and thanked me
for helping Him.
He was
a friend
who loved me like no other.

Ironically, the scribes and Pharisees,
who could not agree on anything else,
did agree about Jesus.
They hated Him and rejected His teachings.
They had even tried to kill Him
in His hometown.[12]

We had withdrawn to the wilderness
east of the Jordan River[13]

when we got word from Bethany
that our friend Lazarus was sick.[14]
Jesus said he was actually dead
and insisted that we return.[15]
A wave of anxiety swept through me.
None of us wanted to go back.
Bethany was
located less than two miles outside Jerusalem,
where we had always faced strong opposition.[16]
Lately the hostility had been becoming more intense.
The closer we got to Jerusalem,
the worse it became.
What Jesus was teaching was radical.
If He was right,
the scribes were wrong.
And these were not gentle
discussions characterized by mutual respect.
These were high-stakes arguments.[17]
The scribes and Pharisees said
Jesus was wrong,
that we were all traitors,
leading Israel away from God.
They accused Jesus of being from
the ancient evil,
that liar,
who had convinced humans
to turn away from God.

This
accusation
filled Jesus with disgust
at what evil had done to humanity,
and the scribes became His bitter enemy.
There were rumors of a plot
to have Jesus killed.[18]
The last time we were in Jerusalem,

the crowd,
instigated by the scribes,
had started heckling Jesus as He taught,
spitting on Him
and shouting insults.
They started throwing rocks at us,[19]
forcing us to run for our lives,
to hide in the wilderness.

Despite the danger in Jerusalem,
Jesus calmly stated
His intention
to go back
to Bethany.
A sense of dread filled us all.
Bracing myself,
I spoke up.
"Let's go too,"
I said.
"We might as well die with Him."[20]

When we arrived in Bethany,
Lazarus had been in the tomb four days.[21]
A crowd had gathered,
some from Jerusalem.
Jesus
broke down and cried.

Then,
in utter contempt for the evil
that had brought death and suffering to earth,
He demanded
we move the stone.
Jesus shouted for Lazarus to come out of the tomb.
Still wrapped in his burial cloth,
the dead man walked out.[22]

Everyone cheered and shouted.
News spread quickly to Jerusalem.
The Sadducees,
who taught there was no life after death,[23]
were outraged.
They frantically
told anyone who would listen that
this was not reasonable,
not even possible;
that this was a simple magic trick[24]
performed by two close friends.

We had fled to Ephraim,[25]
fifteen miles to the north.[26]
A week had passed
and it was already time to go back to Bethany
on our way to Jerusalem
to celebrate Passover.
We all knew the authorities
would be waiting to arrest us in Bethany.
And now, new threats
to kill both Jesus and Lazarus arose.[27]

The laughter and fellowship by the campfire were gone,
replaced
by tension and bickering.
When we got to Bethany,
everyone was still talking about Lazarus,[28]
and many were now saying
Jesus was the Messiah.[29]
The next morning,
Lazarus,
the twelve of us,
some of the women, and Jesus
all left Bethany together to walk to the temple.
Jerusalem was filling up with thousands of visitors

Jesus had been traveling and teaching
throughout the region
for almost three years
and was well known.
As we entered the city,
the crowd recognized Jesus
and started cheering Him and laying down palm branches.[30]

Later,
the twelve of us
had dinner
alone with Jesus.
I was expecting to hear
His plan—
how He was going to defeat Rome
and restore Israel.
I hoped
He would ask me to play
an important role
in establishing His new kingdom.

But my anticipation
quickly turned to disappointment.
Judas left abruptly,[31]
and Jesus started talking in riddles,
announcing
that He would be with us
only
a little while longer.[32]
A sense of unease crept through me.
How
could Jesus be the Messiah
and rule Israel
if He wasn't here?
Then Jesus said
that where He was going

we could not follow now.[33]
I grumbled to James
that His words made no sense.
Jesus told us that we should trust God,
that He was leaving to be in God's presence,
in the Kingdom of Heaven,
outside time,
where there are many dwelling places.
Jesus also told us that we should
trust Him
because He was telling us the truth
and that we could join Him later.

Jesus continued
to say that we knew
the way
to this place
where He was going.
I did not know this place.
Irritated,
I blurted out,
"What do you mean, 'We know the way'?"
"We don't even know where You're going,
so how can we know the way?"[34]

Jesus studied me.
He seemed troubled,
but not for Himself.
There was an awkward silence,
and then He told me that
He was the way—
somehow,
He was the path.
And He said that if I really knew Him,
I would know His Father.[35]
I did not understand.

A sense of doom settled over me.
Jesus then assured us that
it was best
that He go,
because a Comforter,
a Spirit of Truth, would be coming,
a Holy Spirit who would always be with us.[36]
I stopped listening.
After dinner
we all went
to the Garden of Gethsemane.
Jesus went off to pray.
I fell asleep.[37]

I awoke to a strange smell.
The night was dark and cold.
I recognized Judas in the shadows.
Roman soldiers were everywhere.
They were arresting Jesus![38]
A Roman soldier,
nostrils flaring,
glared at me,
raised his spear and violently
thrust it at me.
It was as if evil's filthy claw
were reaching out to tear at me.[39]

Terrified,
I couldn't think.
I started running,
I ran as fast
and as far as I could.

Exhausted,
out of breath,
I stumbled and fell.

Then,
I started crawling on my hands and knees,
frantically looking for a place to hide.
Head pounding,
heart pounding,
certain I was about to die,
I doubled over behind some bushes,
whimpering.
I clutched my stomach,
and started to vomit.

The following day,
we should have been at the temple,
sacrificing a lamb,
celebrating Passover.
Instead, the unbelievable had happened.
Jesus had been tried in the middle of the night
and found guilty of blasphemy by the Sanhedrin,[40]
dismissed by Herod Antipas,[41]
beaten by order of Pilate,[42]
and crucified.[43]
By nightfall
He was dead,
and His tomb was being guarded by Roman soldiers.[44]

We disciples all huddled behind locked doors.
The stench of fear and despair was suffocating.
Jesus' mother, Mary,
was sobbing,
inconsolable,
her grief unbearable.
In a single day,
our world had been turned upside down.

The ancient evil,
the liar, had won.

Rome had triumphed.
Death on a Roman cross was final.
Jesus was dead.
Our friend Judas
had betrayed us
then hanged himself.[45]
A few days ago
we were being cheered.
Now,
we were being hunted down like common criminals.
A sickening horror overtook me.
I couldn't think.
I couldn't eat.
I couldn't sleep.
I was exhausted and without hope.

The last few days had been an emotional blur.
That liar,
his small voice
in the back of my mind,
started nagging at me,
taunting me:
"This Jesus was no Messiah.
How could the Messiah
be crucified as a traitor?
Jesus did not defeat Caesar.
Caesar defeated Jesus.
You have been betrayed.
Israel will never be restored.
Save yourself.
Get out.
Go home.
Go back to Galilee."

Early Sunday morning,
Mary Magdalene went to the tomb.

She came running back
to find Peter and John.
Visibly shaken,
crying,
she told them
someone had stolen the body of Jesus.
Peter, John, and Mary
all ran back to the tomb.[46]
Peter and John returned
but Mary stayed behind.[47]
Peter and John
confirmed the Magdalene's report:
The body of Jesus was gone!

Then
Mary burst into the house,
shouting that
she had seen Jesus!
that HE WAS ALIVE![48]
We were all stunned.

The room erupted.
Everyone yelled at once.
This was impossible!
Mary was a grief-stricken crazy woman!
Even if
Jesus were still alive,
why
would He show Himself first to a woman?
Why not to Peter or John?
The room was explosive;
angry disbelief filled the air
I did not believe her.
No one believed her.
I ran outside.
I had had enough!
I was going home!

After buying some
bread, cheese,
and flasks of wine
for my journey home,
I returned
to say good-bye.
When I walked into the house,
everything had changed.
A fresh aroma of life,
energy, and excitement
filled the room.
I was besieged.
They all started coming at me,
crowding around me.
"WE HAVE SEEN HIM!"
"HE'S ALIVE!"
"JESUS WAS HERE!"
"HE BREATHED HIS SPIRIT ON US!"[49]
"HE *IS* THE MESSIAH!"

I was stunned…
That's impossible,
I told myself.
There is no life after death.
This was some kind of magic trick!
I had given up more than two years of my life.
I had left my family.
I had left my friends.
I had been put out of my synagogue.
I had lost everything.
If Jesus were still alive,
How could He forget me?
Why would He have come
when I wasn't there?
What could He have been thinking?
Resentment

twisted inside me.
They all kept rushing at me,
pleading with me to believe.
But I had been betrayed!
Jesus was not the Messiah!
He had been crucified like a common criminal!
He was dead!

A tidal wave of anger and grief
engulfed me.
I pushed them all away
and exploded.
"UNLESS
I SEE
THE NAIL MARKS IN HIS HANDS
AND PUT MY FINGERS
WHERE THE NAILS WERE,
AND PUT MY HAND INTO HIS SIDE,
I AM NOT GOING TO BELIEVE!"[50]
I stormed out of the room
and began walking toward Galilee.

On the third day of my journey,
a great weariness
overcame me.
The day was done;
night was falling.
The shadows of the evening hour
were moving across the sky.
In a secluded spot
off the road
I sat down.
Nothing
had changed:
Rome still ruled;
Antipas still governed Galilee;

the scribes and Pharisees
were still blaming and accusing.

But,
I realized
I had changed,
I was different.
My heart had come to know
a new sort of peace.
I wanted to go back to Jerusalem,
to be with my friends,
but
the liar, the ancient evil,
whispering in my mind,
told me
there was no hope.
After all, he reminded me,
I had bragged that I'd been willing to die with Jesus.
But
when Jesus was arrested,
I had hidden in fear,
gagging on my own vomit.
And on the night He was betrayed,
at our last supper together,
I had asked my senseless,
stupid question.
After two years of Jesus' teachings,
I had learned nothing,
nothing at all.
And now,
I refused to believe.
I was no better than the scribes and Pharisees,
always demanding signs,
always questioning,
never believing.
For me, there was no hope.

I wanted to go away
from everything
and everyone.
I wanted to die.
Instead,
I lay down
and cried until I slept.

But at dawn,
I was given the sense
that there was hope.
I was not to listen to the liar.
Instead, I was reminded of God's love,
a love that existed before the ancient evil,
before creation,
before the dawn of time;
a love so strong,
a love so powerful,
that it holds the universe together.
It told me to
listen to my heart.
I knew I had
to go back to Jerusalem.

When I arrived
I had been gone more than a week.[51]
Tired, filthy, hungry,
I hesitated,
watching from a distance,
doubting myself.
Maybe…,
they won't want me back.
Then
I was spotted.
They all rushed out to me,
greeted me,

urged me to come inside.
I resisted,
but they pulled me in
and locked the door.[52]
Everyone was glad to see me.
They offered me some broiled fish, bread, wine.
Everything was happening so fast.
Everyone was laughing, talking.
Then,
the room became strangely quiet.
The others started backing away from me.
I could feel a Presence.
Someone had entered the room.

And I knew
that this Someone
had come for me.
I was alone,
no family,
no friends,
no high priest to stand with me.

And I knew this Someone
was not a
high-minded,
distant, unfeeling God
who watched others suffer from a distance.
He had entered our world,
become human,
become one of us.
He had made the ultimate sacrifice.
He had shed His own blood.
He had earned
the right to judge me.
This encounter
was an intensely personal moment

for the two of us.
And I,
weak,
cowardly,
unbelieving,
was about to be judged.
How could I have been so wrong?
The Lion of Judah
was going to pounce on me,
drag me away,
and tear me to pieces!

I noticed a fierce
hammering in my heart.
My hands were shaking,
my knees trembling.
I stumbled to my feet and turned to face Him.
He was standing in front of me.
I could barely look.
His appearance was terrifying.
He was beautiful—beyond belief

He held out His hands to me.
The wounds were still there.
He told me to put my finger
where the nails had been.
Utterly overwhelmed,
I started to cry.
I could not move.
He told me to put my hand into His side,
but I could not move.
My mind
could not comprehend what was happening—
the inconceivable,
the incomprehensible,
the impossible—

was true.
The God of Abraham and Moses,
the one true God of the universe
was my Friend.

Jesus told me to stop doubting and to believe.[53]
Immediately, I believed in my heart.[54]
I dropped to my knees, and
I struggled to speak through my tears,
"My Lord and my God."[55]
Jesus had searched my heart—
examined my mind—
and found faith.[56]
He told the others that,
because I had seen Him,
I had believed.
Then He added,
"Blessed are those who have not seen
yet believe."[57]

He reached down and put His hand on my shoulder.
So much love,
so strong,
so powerful,
that with each beat of my heart,
I felt a surge of energy.

I was bursting with love and pure joy,
unable to contain myself.
I felt lighter than air;
I seemed
to be floating.
His grace overflowed.
His spirit shone.
His quiet majesty
filled the room with God's glory.

I felt completely safe.
For the first time in my life
I was at peace with God
in heart and mind.

And what does this all mean to you?
Today,
that liar
the ancient evil,
is nagging at *you*,
whispering to *you*,
that the events of two thousand years ago are
distant,
vague,
and irrelevant.
But
know this:
Two thousand years ago
something happened to me,
and to almost one hundred other[58]
uneducated,
pitiful,
and leaderless people.
That something
was the Holy Spirit.
He touched our hearts,
and that moment was so overwhelming,
so powerful,
it has changed the world.
Do not listen
to the wisdom
of twenty-first century dying men.
Listen to your heart.
The Spirit of the living God,
who revealed Himself to you.
through His Son Jesus,

is at work in your heart,
urging you to choose hope and life.
He is the last hope of earth,
the only hope of mankind,
and He wants you to know
He loves you.

Amen.

(As Thomas starts to leave, someone from the audience calls out, "What did Jesus look like?" Thomas turns, pauses, and speaks.)

Some said He was too tall,
but others said He was too short.
Some thought He was too dark-skinned,
but others said He was too fair-skinned.
Some said His hair was too long,
but others thought His hair was too short.
I think when you see Him,
you'll agree with me,
He looks just right.

Then Thomas adds.
"God's story has a beginning, a middle, and an end.
The prophet Moses will come to tell you about the beginning.
The apostle Paul is going to tell you about the middle,
and the disciple John will come to tell you about how it's going to end.

(Thomas leaves.)

Chapter 6

The Prophet Moses
"I Am Has Sent Me"

Moses said to God, "Suppose I go to the Israelites and say to them, 'The God of your fathers has sent me to you,' and they ask me, 'What is his name?' Then what shall I tell them?"

God said to Moses, "I AM WHO I AM. This is what you are to say to the Israelites: I AM has sent me to you" (Exodus 3:13-14, NIV).

I am the prophet,
the man,
Moses.
I was born
thirty-five hundred years ago[1]
in the delta region of Egypt[2]
to Hebrew slaves
Amran and Jochebed.[3]
I have stepped from God's space,
the kingdom of heaven,
into your space,
Earth,
to tell you my story.
I was born a slave
but raised a prince.
I was a shepherd,
meek and mild,
but also a ruthless warrior.

At times
I was strong and heroic
but at other times
timid and tortured with self-doubt.[4]

I wrote,
dictated,
and helped edit the first five books of the Bible.
In the last two hundred years
modern skeptics
have not only questioned
if I wrote those books,
but they are now questioning
my mortal existence.[5]
The truth of my existence
can be found in your DNA
which bears the indelible imprint of all human history
going back to Adam and Eve.[6]
There are more than six billion people on Earth today,
the majority of whom are in some way affected
by the relationship
I had with "I AM,"
the one true God of the universe.[7]

Before I begin my story,
please stand that we might pray.

"Deliver Us"

God of Abraham,
Isaac, and Jacob,
You are the great I AM.
We come before you now,
Wanting to walk in Your truth.

Yahweh,
Will You hear our prayer?

We cry out to You.
We want to hear Your voice.
Deliver us, Yahweh.
Yahweh.

Rise up, O Mighty God.
Deliver us today.
Our back is against the wall.
We cannot run away.
There's nowhere to hide.
By Your blood You've made for us the way.

Yahweh,
Will You hear our prayer?
We cry out to You.
We want to hear Your voice.
Deliver us, Yahweh.
Yahweh.

Amen

Egypt was the most powerful nation in the world
with a population of almost four million,[8]
dependent on the Nile River,
with plenty of food and water.[9]
To keep the Nile flowing,
the people of Egypt worshiped
more than two thousand different gods.[10]
They made images of these gods from wood and stone,
and built temples for them.[11]

Pharaoh ruled Egypt
with absolute and total control.
His slightest whim or most trivial comment
was not questioned.[12]
Pharaoh was believed to be

the son of Amun-Re,[13]
the supreme god of Egypt.
Pharaoh was the
mediator between the people of Egypt,
Amun-Re, and the other gods.[14]
At night Amun-Re
would make the journey
through the dark underworld of the Red Sea,
overcoming Apropos,
the God of Chaos,
so that the sun would come up in the morning.[15]

In Pharaoh's crown
was the serpent Wadjet,
who protected Pharaoh.[16]

Pharaoh,
concerned about the Israelites becoming too dangerous,
made us slaves.[17]
Abusing his power,
Pharaoh tried to kill us off with crushing workloads,
forcing us to leave our dead
fathers, sons, and brothers
unburied at worksites.[18]
That failed
to keep us from growing stronger.
So Pharaoh ordered the midwives
to strangle newborn males as they were born.[19]
That failed too, and
the evil behind Pharaoh
ordered more violence,
the systematic genocide
of God's chosen people.[20]
All male babies were to be thrown
into the Nile River
and drowned.[21]

That is when I was born.
At great risk
my mother hid me for three months,
but finally had to cast me adrift on the Nile
in an ark of bulrushes,
dabbed with pitch and slime.[22]
A daughter of Pharaoh, Thermuthis,[23]
took compassion on me,
and I became her son, a prince of
Egypt.[24]
Pharaoh hardly noticed.
He had many wives,
hundreds of sons and daughters,
and more than five hundred servants.[25]
As a young boy
I had difficulty in speaking,
I was lonely,
and I lived in the constant fear of being discovered.
I compensated
by working harder and studying harder than the others,
excelling in the new skills of reading and writing.[26]

As a young man,
I led Pharaoh's army against the Ethiopians
and earned a decisive victory,[27]
but became feared by the Egyptians
and made enemies of many of them.[28]
When I saw an Egyptian taskmaster
savagely beating a helpless Hebrew slave,
I stepped in and killed the Egyptian.
Afraid,
I buried him.[29]
Others saw me,
and my enemies
spread word
about what I had done.

Pharaoh heard and ordered that
I be hunted down and killed.[30]
I fled into the wilderness.
No longer a settled prince of Egypt,
I faced never-ending change,
always looking for food and water,
enduring heat and cold
and relentless dust and grime—
hardships meant to test
what was in my heart.[31]

I settled in Midian,[32]
and became a simple shepherd.[33]
During the night
I tended my flocks in solitude.
The stars,
too numerous to count,
overwhelmed me.
I could not grasp the size and scope of the heavens.[34]
My heart searched for answers.

Something was deeply wrong.[35]
What was my purpose?
When did I become self-conscious?
When did I become aware that I was alive and that I would die?[36]

Our fathers had told us of a former time,
long, long ago,
before my time,[37]
that the one true God of the universe
created humans in His own image.
We were the pinnacle of His creation,
the center of His love.[38]
God gave mankind dominion over His creation.
He gave man rule over all creatures,
all plants,
and everything on earth that has the breath of life.[39]

But,
a second will,
a non-human, non-divine will,
bent on undermining God's creation in general,
and humans in particular,[40]
forced its way into eternity.
The ancient evil,
rebelled against God.[41]
Seeking absolute and total control,
evil lied to and finally convinced the two humans on earth,
Adam and Eve,
to turn away from God.
After Adam and Eve
how long did it take mankind
to turn completely away from God?[42]
Did humans resist at all
or did it take thousands of years
before their resistance was worn away?
Where was God?[43]

The mystery
of why and how this cosmic struggle came about
we did not know,
and perhaps we were incapable of understanding.[44]
The results we did know.
Because evil is present,
God seems to be absent.
Evil now exists
in a carefully restricted area of creation, Earth.[45]
Becoming more and more separated from God,
through a succession of choices,
mankind turned inward to self,
became increasingly corrupt,
leading to violence and
increasing death and suffering
in the world.[46]
It seemed hopeless.

Against all hope,
one man,
my ancestor,
Abram from Ur of the Chaldeans,
had faith and believed in God.

God changed his name to Abraham
and made an everlasting covenant with him
for all generations to come
that He would make him a great nation
and through his seed
all the people on earth would be blessed.[47]

But,
we had been slaves four hundred years,
being ravaged by Pharaoh.
Where was this God of Abraham?
Was he far off,
remote and controlling
like the Egyptian gods?[48]
My heart searched for answers,
but no answers came.
I had become an old man,
a husband and
a father,
living in peaceful solitude,
expecting to quietly end my days.

But,
my story did not end there.
It was just the beginning.
I had gone to the far side of the desert
to Mt. Horeb with my flock.[49]
What happened next
would change the destiny of my people
and the history of the world.[50]

A strange appearance—
about twenty yards away—
a bush,
strangely burning but not burning up.
A blinding white light was close by,
inside
and all around the bush.
I was paralyzed with fear.
I heard a great voice
unlike any other voice I had ever heard
like a thundering waterfall.

The voice called my name.
I let out a sharp cry.
With great gasps
I tried to recover my breath.
I was told not to approach
for it was holy ground
where the kingdom of heaven and earth intersected.[51]

The voice said that He was the God of my ancestor Abraham.
He wanted me
to go to the new pharaoh
to bring His people out of Egypt,
back to Mt. Horeb
and to the land
He had promised Abraham.
I asked,
"Who should I say has sent me?"
The voice answered,
"Tell them, 'I AM has sent me.'"[52]
I was eighty years old,
Clumsy in speech,
with no army.
Why would the pharaoh listen to me?
I asked God to send someone else.

He gave me a staff,
said that He would always be with me,
and told me to go.[53]

My brother Aaron and I confronted Pharaoh,
demanding that he let our people go.[54]
Pharaoh was outraged,
accused us of being lazy,
and increased our workload.[55]

God started bringing down plague after plague on Egypt—
frogs, boils, hail, locust, darkness.[56]

With each plague,
a different Egyptian god was defeated.
But Pharaoh refused to repent.
He haggled endlessly and pointlessly,
and with each plague
his heart hardened more and more.[57]
Egypt was reduced to a nightmare
of complete chaos.

Fear gripped the entire country.
Pharaoh hated me.
Even the Israelites turned against me.[58]
I went to see Pharaoh for a final time.
Frustrated,
angry,
his authority challenged,
he vented his rage at me.
"GET OUT OF MY SIGHT!" he roared.
"THE DAY YOU SEE MY FACE AGAIN,
YOU WILL DIE!"[59]

Then,
the final plague—

all of Egypt's firstborn
were to die.
But,
the firstborn of Israel
would be passed over
by sacrificing a lamb
and spreading its blood over our doorways.[60]
It was a long,
dark night of terror.
Listening to the cries of the Egyptians,
waiting,
not knowing when or where
death might strike them.
After that dreadful night,
Pharaoh agreed to let us go.[61]

I divided the people into twelve tribes
and began to organize our exodus.
It was a daunting task.
Hundreds of thousands of men, women, children
plus livestock
and all their belongings,
needing food and water.[62]

It would take several weeks
to walk back to Mt. Horeb.
We moved slowly,
traveling day and night,
walking five hours then resting seven.[63]

I could hear a slight rumble
coming from the west.
Strangely,
instead of going the most direct route
to Mt. Horeb,
God directed me to go south.[64]

I was worried.
It didn't make sense.
We had reached a dead end
and set up a vast encampment
next to what you call today the Gulf of Aqaba,
part of the Red Sea.[65]
The rumble to the west
was growing.
I could see a huge dust cloud in the distance.
Uneasiness was spreading through the camp.
What was it?
Who was it?

When Pharaoh realized what he had done,
he changed his mind.[66]
He called up his chariots and all his army.
Pharaoh's chariots were unstoppable,
feared and detested,
weapons of mass destruction.[67]
It was unmistakable.
Pharaoh,
the son of the supreme god of Egypt
Amun-Re,
Wadjet the serpent in his crown,
six-hundred chariots,
thousands of horses,
and two-hundred-fifty thousand men
were relentlessly bearing down on us
at full gait.[68]
The rumble to the west
grew to a thundering roar.

We were defenseless slaves, women and children.
We had no weapons.
Panic set in.
The Red Sea was at our backs.

It was more than one-and-a-half miles across
and more than two hundred feet deep.[69]
This was where Apropos,
the Egyptian god of chaos, ruled.
We were trapped
and faced certain death!
The men turned all their hatred at me.
"LET'S GO BACK TO EGYPT!" they shouted.
"BETTER TO BE SLAVES THAN DIE HERE IN THE
WILDERNESS!"[70]
Chaos and confusion took over.
Sheer terror engulfed us.
There was no hope!
I raised my staff.

There was one hope!
"DO NOT BE AFRAID!" I called out.
"STAND FIRM
AND YOU WILL SEE THE DELIVERANCE
THE LORD WILL BRING YOU TODAY!"[71]
The waters of the Red Sea were divided
and we walked across on dry ground
to safety.
An angry Pharaoh followed us.
I stretched out my hand, and
the waters returned.
Pharaoh and all his army
were completely destroyed.[72]
God crushed the evil behind Pharaoh,
Amun-Re,
Wadjet the Serpent,
Apropos,
and all the two-thousand false gods of Egypt.
Now the people of the world would know
it is "I AM" who is
the one and only true God of the Universe.[73]

The bodies of the Egyptians
washed up on shore
and we collected their weapons.[74]

We would need them
as we headed into the wilderness
into the Desert of Shur
to Mt. Horeb.[75]
The Israelites had romanticized
what it would be like to be free,
but I had been here
forty years earlier,
fleeing from Pharaoh.
I knew how difficult it would be.

The Israelites
were confused,
unsettled,
and angry.[76]
The Amalekites attacked
our faint and weary stragglers.[77]
God was no longer
going to allow us to be passive observers,
standing by and watching.

The transformation
from slaves to a nation was to begin.
We were now to join the fight
along with God.
My leadership was constantly questioned.
There were losses and pain,
but the outcome was certain,[78]
and the Amalekites were defeated.[79]

In the third month
after leaving Egypt,

we arrived at Mt. Horeb.[80]
I went up to the mountain
and received God's law.
This law is the foundation
for all mankind
to live in harmony and justice.
When I returned,
the people had made a golden calf,
and were worshiping it.[81]

I was furious!
God had just brought us out of Egypt.
We were His people,
chosen to lead the nations back to the one true God.

We were not to make images of false gods;
God had made us in His image!
We were not to build temples for those false gods;
God had built us a temple,
Earth![82]
I made them burn the golden calf
grind it up,
put it in their water
and drink it.[83]

Embarrassed,
hurt,
and humiliated,
I pleaded with God,
asking His forgiveness.
I had failed as a leader
and wanted to quit.[84]
God would not let me give up
and ordered me to go back
to lead His people to the Promised Land.[85]
Later,

I went to Mt. Horeb again
where I spent forty days and
was directed to start writing down[86]
God's covenant as expressed in
the Ten Commandments.

When I came down the mountain
my face had changed.[87]
The others were afraid
and stood a distance from me,
gasping in horror.[88]
I started to wear a veil.[89]
My leadership became mysterious and scary.[90]
Hiding behind the veil
made me feel safe and powerful.

We arrived at Kadesh,
south of Canaan.
The trip had been difficult.
These Israelites were not grateful,
were not obedient,
nor trusting the God who freed them.

Instead,
they grumbled,
were rebellious,
and complained bitterly about everything.[91]
I sent out a group of scouts
to explore the Promised Land.[92]
They reported the land was beautiful
but the people were strong,
fierce,
and warlike.
Some of the scouts
advised we should not attempt
to take the land.[93]

The people reacted bitterly
"WHY HAVE YOU BROUGHT US HERE?
BETTER TO DIE IN EGYPT!"
Joshua and Caleb pleaded with the people
not to be afraid
and to trust in God.
But the people refused to listen
and started looking for someone
to lead them back to Egypt![94]
Aaron and I were distraught.[95]
The price for their fear of failure
and lack of trust in God
was forty years in the wilderness![96]

Our destiny had been interrupted.
We would have to revisit the wilderness
and reclaim the wisdom of our ancestor Abraham
before becoming a nation.[97]

After forty long years
that great and terrible experience[98] in the wilderness
came to an end.
We had been sifted and sorted[99]
by a patient and loving God.
In the wilderness
we had learned to trust and hope in God,
to love one another,
and to search for God with all our hearts
and with all our minds.[100]
What God was asking of Israel was not too difficult—[101]
offer our free obedience,
to love Him,
and to keep His commands.[102]

God set before us the choice of life or death,
urging us to choose life.[103]

Israel was now ready
to enter the Promised Land.

I pleaded with God to let me go into the Promised Land[104]
but was told no.
I stood alone on a hill,[105]
overlooking the people of Israel one final time,
as they moved off into the distance,
creating a huge cloud of dust.

We had been tested and
endured many hardships together.
As each tribe approached,
the people dropped their standard.
We looked on each other
with bowed heads,
some crying as they silently passed by.
My heart was breaking.
Never again
in this place or time
would I have one of my grandchildren
on my knee,
or tell stories and laugh with my friends.
I could hear
cheering and singing off in the distance.
In thirty days
Joshua would lead them to the Promised Land.[106]
I was worried.

It was a huge responsibility
to lead the world back to God,[107]
and these were a stiff-necked,
stubborn people.[108]
I realized
the future was in doubt.[109]
What if Israel failed?

What was God's plan?
I had to place my trust in God.

As for me,
my time was over.[110]
I never expected to encounter the God I met forty years earlier.

The greatness of God
had aroused fear in me
but His goodness and mercy
encouraged me not to be afraid.[111]

He was an intimate,
direct-dealing,
uncontrolling,
and forgiving God,
who asked for my free obedience
and to be my partner.[112]

God knew
it was time
to take off the veil that
I had been hiding behind all my life.
I did not want others to know
my insecurities,
my pain,
my failures.[113]
Our face expresses who we are.
It was my deepest desire,
to be face to face before God,
but I now realized,
because of humans turning away from God inside time on earth,
this could happen only outside of time.[114]

God showed me
that I needed to be something

I could hardly put into words—
to be my true self,[115]
take off my veil,
to be a part of and see
face-to-face
the glory of God.[116]
Instead of entering the Promised Land
I was unveiled
and stood face to face before God in eternity.
God did not turn away.

I was united with
and bathed in His glory.
I did not get what I asked for
but I was given more than I had ever hoped for.
God bent down
raised me up on His wings,[117]
bore me on the breath of dawn,
made me to shine like the sun,
and held me in the palm of His hand.[118]

May that same God,
the God of Abraham,
the one true God of the Universe,
bless you and keep you,
make His face to shine upon you,
be gracious to you
and give you peace.[119]

Amen.

Chapter 7

The Apostle Paul
God's Secret Plan

"God's secret plan has now been revealed to us; it is a plan centered on Christ, designed long ago according to his good pleasure. And this is the plan: At the right time he will bring everything together under the authority of Christ—everything in heaven and on earth" (Ephesians 1:9-10 NLT).

I am Saul of Tarsus,[1]
known today
by many of you
as the apostle Paul.
Two thousand years ago
I was
murderous and hateful,
an enemy of God.[2]
I persecuted and ravaged His people.[3]
But then,
I was chosen by God
for His historical purpose,[4]
to proclaim to the world
that Jesus of Nazareth
is the Messiah,
the Son of God.
It was Jesus
not Caesar,
who was king of the world.[5]

I am here to explain
God's plan,
a plan that has been unfolding over thousands of years.

It is God's plan to defeat the ancient evil,
to redeem and re-create His creation.[6]

Before I begin,
please stand for prayer.

"Show Us Your Love"

Lord, here we are
Down on our knees,
Crying out, come and rescue me.

Lord, live in us
And be in all we do.
Show us Your love
That we might love You

Lord, we're sorry
For the things we have done.
We've nowhere to turn
And nowhere to run.
Look upon us, Father,
Hide us in Your Son.
Wash us in His blood
And let Your kingdom come.

Lord, we fall on Your mercy.
Lord, we count on Your grace.
For when we did not love You,
You reached down to us,
And we ran to Your embrace

Amen.

I was born a Jew,
in the city of Tarsus in Cilicia,[7]
twelve miles inland from the Mediterranean Sea,
in the country you know today as Turkey.
Tarsus was a busy metropolis,
a crossroads between Rome and the Orient.
A city of many different cultures
and international commerce.[8]
I could speak both Greek and Aramaic
and had a working
knowledge of Latin.[9]
My Jewish upbringing was very strict.
I was an outstanding scholar,
well-advanced of my peers in my passion and zeal for Judaism,[10]
knowing the Scriptures inside and out.[11]
I became a Pharisee
in the Shammite tradition,[12]
the strictest,
most zealous sect of our faith.[13]
I passionately believed that
we, Israel,
were the chosen people of God.
God had spoken directly to my ancestors
and we had been entrusted with His Law,
given to us by Moses.[14]
But, now,
Israel was in crisis,
oppressed,
enslaved by the evil of Rome.
I was convinced
that God was going to act in history,
send the Messiah,
and liberate us from Rome.

Professionally I was moving toward membership
on the ruling council,

the Sanhedrin.
It would then be my responsibility
to take
zealous,
severe,
even violent action
to ensure the strict observance of God's law
as taught by the scribes.
Such obedience, I was convinced,
would turn God's wrath
away from Israel.[15]
Then,
as prophesied by Isaiah,
God would send the Messiah
to inflict His wrath and fierce anger on our enemies.[16]

A year ago,
a rebel prophet,
Jesus of Nazareth,
who had caused a disturbance in Jerusalem,
was crucified by the Romans.
His followers
were stirring up the people in Jerusalem
in a place called Solomon's Colonnade.[17]
Those believers,
a motley group of
uneducated peasants and fishermen,
were very committed followers of this Jesus.
Of one heart and mind,[18]
they made up a strange story
that this Jesus had been raised from the dead,
that He was the Messiah.
That declaration was
treasonous!
Jesus was a mere carpenter from Nazareth,
an insignificant village of two or three hundred people

in Galilee.[19]
What possible good
could come out of a place like Nazareth?[20]

We brought their leader,
Peter,
before the high priest Caiaphas
and the council of elders[21]
in order to put him to death.[22]
And this Peter,
this fisherman,
condemned us!
He said that Jesus,
whom we had crucified,
was the Messiah,
and that God had raised Him from the dead.[23]
The council was enraged!
But,
one respected leader,
Gamaliel,
warned the council
that if Peter were acting as a man,
he would fail.
But,
if Peter's actions were of God,
he could not be stopped.
By trying to stop him,
Gamaliel reasoned,
we would be enemies of God.[24]
So the council had Peter
flogged,
then released.[25]
I was incensed!
This simple fisherman
was speaking blasphemy!
He should have been stoned and killed.

The Messiah
would be a cosmic figure
sent from God
to overthrow our enemies.[26]
This Jesus
was a traitor
who died on a Roman cross like a common criminal.
He could not be the Messiah!
I had never hated like I hated those people!
I zealously
started rounding up believers,
men and women,
dragging them from their homes,
helping to put about two thousand in jail[27]
and some to death.[28]

One of the most persuasive of the believers
was Stephen.
We arranged for witnesses
to come before the council
and lie about Stephen,
saying that he had spoken
against Moses and the law.[29]
Hearing this testimony,
the people became enraged,
shook their fists,
and shouted.
They rushed at Stephen
and dragged him out of the city
to stone him.
Stephen was taken to the edge of a cliff,
his hands bound.
Someone yelled,
"What are we waiting for?"
Another yelled,
"This is God's will!"

And still another,
"Make it quick!"

As I watched over their garments,[30]
some of the men
lifted Stephen up
and hurled him down onto the rocks below.[31]
He struggled to his knees.
He seemed at peace.
The mob started to chant,
"KILL HIM! KILL HIM! KILL HIM!"
The first rock missed.
A second rock,
thrown with full force,
struck Stephen in the chest
with a sickening thud.
There was a ripple of applause.
He shuddered,
letting out a barely audible sound,
asking God to forgive us![32]
Another rock struck him,
full force,
on the skull.
A chill of pleasure
ran up my spine.
"Yes! Good!" I thought to myself.
Stephen slumped to the ground.
The crowd,
sensing the kill,
closed in.
Their faces were
distorted with hate.
A cascade of rocks
 pounded the defenseless Stephen.
Blood spattered everywhere,
and soon his body was little more

than a shapeless mass of bloody flesh.
When it was over,
the crowd dispersed,
and I returned to my daily routine.[33]

However, the persecutions did not stop the followers of Jesus.
Our attacks had the opposite effect,
scattering them from Jerusalem,
where they continued to speak their heresies.[34]
I obtained permission to go to Damascus
to stop these traitors.

On the road to Damascus,
everything I believed,
everything I had ever been taught,
everything I cared about,
was turned upside down,
inside out.
A light from heaven,
brighter than the sun,
suddenly
blazed around me,[35]
and I was knocked to the ground.
No one—
Nothing had hit me!
The force of the light itself leveled me.
I was utterly overwhelmed.
A still small voice spoke to me.
"SAUL, SAUL, WHY DO YOU PERSECUTE ME?"[36]
Then I saw Him.
Pulse pounding,
gasping for air,
my voice choked with emotion,
I asked who He was.
He said He was Jesus.[37]
My heart cracked.

Horrified,
I thought the end was near.[38]

Then,
He said that
I had been chosen
to be His witness to all people,
Jews and non-Jews,
to turn them away from the liar, the ancient evil,
and back to the one true God of the Universe.[39]
Blind,
confused,
paralyzed with fear,
I had to muster all my strength
to stand up
and be led into town.

Full of uncertainty,
unable to grasp what had happened to me,
I did not eat or drink for three days.[40]
I had never met or even seen Jesus.[41]
The Romans were good at killing people by crucifixion.
Jesus was dead.
How could He be alive?
This was not my imagination,
not a hallucination,
not a ghost.[42]
This was a real body
that had come out of the tomb,
the body of one who had been dead more than a year.[43]
I knew this was Jesus.
Somehow He had a new transformed body,
resurrected,
imperishable,[44]
a new physicality.[45]
A local man,

Ananias,
had been told by God to find me,
to restore my sight,
and to emphasize to me again
what I had been told three days earlier:[46]
God had chosen me
to know His will
to see the Messiah,
and to hear the words of God
directly from His mouth.
I was to be His witness to all people.[47]

But how could this be?
I was an enemy of God.
How could I be chosen?
The things I had done—
The horrors of my past.
I could not forget the ghastly images of torture and pain
I had inflicted on others.
It should have been hopeless for me.
I had no defense for what I had done.
Yet Jesus searched my heart—
and found it not to be hardened.
Jesus examined my mind—
and found it not to be closed.
In these truths there was hope for me.
By God's grace and unlimited love,
my obedience in the wrong direction
was not counted against me.[48]
Murderous and hateful,
less deserving of God's mercy and grace than the least of men,[49]
I was nevertheless forgiven.

When the Jews in Damascus
heard what had happened to me
they wanted to kill me.[50]

I fled for my life
to Mt. Sinai in Arabia,[51]
and stayed there
for the next three years.[52]
It was an agonizing time.
I was forced
to go deep inside myself to
places I had never been before.
The exercise was confusing,
painful,
trying to sort out
where I had gone so wrong.
I had been so sure of my judgments.
I had never imagined
Peter and Stephen,
who had followed Jesus,
were right—
and I was wrong!

God had forgiven me,
but I was not free.
I wept until I cried out all my guilt.
With the help of the Comforter,
the Holy Spirit,
I rethought everything
and gave up my long-held beliefs,[53]
about Israel
and about the Messiah.
Relying on my education and knowledge of the Old Testament
Scriptures,
I worked backward
from my encounter with Jesus
on the road to Damascus[54]
to determine where and how I had gone so wrong.
I went back to the beginning,
back to Adam and Eve,

who, persuaded by the ancient evil,
had turned away from God.[55]
Later, against all hope,
Abraham had chosen faith and believed in God,
and God had made a binding covenant with Abraham
that through his seed all the nations of the earth
would be blessed.[56]
Then God sent Moses
to lead the people of Israel
out of Egypt,
entrusting them with His law, and
giving them the Promised Land,
so they could be God's light to the world.[57]
But,
the ancient evil,
ruthless and determined,
twisted the law,
causing Israel to turn inward.
Israel failed to be a light to the world.[58]

Now,
fifteen hundred years after we received the law,
Caesar,
not Israel,
ruled the world.
We Jews
had become nothing but a
small,
strange,
troublesome religious people among many.[59]
We had turned inward,
strictly observing the law as taught by the scribes,
waiting for God to send the Messiah.
Caesar governed more than sixty million people.[60]
And after Julius Caesar,
Roman emperors

were called
"sons of God."
They had the power to sweep aside all opposition,
the power to create a new world order,
an order that offered peace,
harmony,
and unity to the world.[61]
Like Egypt's Pharaoh long ago,
with his mingling of politics and religion,
the evil behind Caesar had absolute and total control
and he demanded to be hailed as king of the world.[62]
Abusing his power just as Pharaoh had,
Caesar
bought peace at the terrible price of
unrelenting,
violent,
oppressive force.
Rome's symbol of authority was the cross:
"Repent and worship mighty Rome –
or die on the cross."[63]

First,
Adam and Eve had
turned away from God.
Then,
Israel had failed God.
And now—
Jesus had been crucified like a common criminal.
The ancient evil had triumphed again.
The entire universe was suffering and groaning
under the burden of the evil.[64]

So was God's creation a gigantic blunder?
Had His plan for the universe been destroyed?
God could not rescind His covenant with Abraham.[65]
It seemed like an impossible situation.

Had evil triumphed?
Why didn't the all-powerful God stop all this suffering
and just start His plan for history over again?
Because,
God's secret plan is not to destroy
and start over again
but to redeem
and re-create.[66]
His plan—
brilliant
and breathtaking—
is unfolding over thousands of years.
God will
fully expose
to all the universe
the consequences,
the death and the suffering,
that continues to come
from turning away from Him.
In this way,
God's unlimited love and wisdom
will be made known to all people
and throughout His creation.[67]
When I understood
for the first time
that God's plan
was something more spectacular
than I had ever imagined,
I was overcome with unspeakable joy.
The wisdom and scope of His plan
brought me to my knees.[68]

Consider
the depths of the wisdom of God!
He has done the impossible
in one daring and climactic move.

His secret plan
was to send His Son
Jesus
as the Messiah,
as Abraham's seed,
as Israel's anointed representative.[69]
Jesus offered the obedience
that Adam and Eve did not offer.
Jesus offered the obedience to God
that Israel could not offer.[70]
Jesus was perfect.
The ancient evil could not confuse Him,
evil could not trick Him,
evil never dwelt in Him.[71]
The one man,
Jesus the Messiah,
took on the punishment
for the evil of all mankind,
the evil that came from the actions of one man, Adam.

God split the
re-creation of the world into two phases.
Jesus' victory over death on the Roman cross
signaled the beginning of the first phase:
the release of God's Holy Spirit into the world
to begin the remaking of creation.[72]
Isaiah had prophesied a warrior-king
to free the universe from evil,
but he also predicted
a suffering servant
who would be oppressed and afflicted,
brought as a Passover lamb to slaughter.[73]
As a young,
zealous Pharisee,
I had not realized
it was the evil in me—and the evil within all humans—

that the Messiah would die for.
In addition, Isaiah had foretold
that God's blessing would be for all people,
for Jews and non-Jews alike.

So the first phase of re-creation has begun.
Accepting Jesus as the Messiah,
the Son of God,
you become part of the new family of God,[74]
indwelt with God's Holy Spirit,
receiving the gift of life,[75]
and helping Him with His re-creation efforts here on Earth.[76]
Therefore,
you can work and you must work,
now—
to help with this re-creation
and in anticipation of that day to come
when Jesus returns.
No prayer offered today,
No act of kindness extended today,
No act of love lived out today,
is ever in vain.[77]
God sees. God blesses. God re-creates through you.

The second phase of God's re-creation—
the return of His Son Jesus to earth,
and the liberation of all creation from evil—
is yet to come.[78]

Meanwhile,
evil—
vigorous,
determined, unrelenting,
always stalking,
always looking for weakness,
still seeking absolute and total control on earth—

continues to spread death and suffering,
continues to turn humans away from God.

I requested prayer[79] that
I fearlessly proclaim that Jesus,
not Caesar,
was king of the world, and
God enabled me to do so
for thirty years.
I faced opposition everywhere
and from everyone,
Jews and Romans alike.
So I was constantly on the move,
going to unknown, unsafe places,
repeatedly arrested.
Shipwrecked three times,
spending a day and a night
on the open sea.
Flogged five times,
stripped and beaten three times,[80]
stoned and left for dead in Lystra.[81]
In Jerusalem,
forty men
took a solemn oath
not to eat or drink
until they killed me.[82]

In A.D. 64
the city of Rome burned for more than a week.[83]
Because of our refusal to worship him,[84]
Nero blamed the followers of Jesus,
for setting the fire.
The ancient evil
used the extreme violence in Rome
to punish us believers.
You never know how

strong your faith is
until you face death for your beliefs.[85]

By order of Nero,
Peter was crucified,[86]
and I was put in prison.
While there,
I heard of
my friends being crucified,
fed to the lions in the Colosseum,
or smeared with pitch and burned alive
to illuminate the emperor's parties at night.
The persecution was so vicious and cruel that
even the citizens of Rome were alarmed.[87]

The ancient evil,
intense in his hatred and fear of God,
is evident today
even in your time.
His assault continues two thousand years later.
Evil stalks the planet even today.

Consider the holocaust,
the killing fields of Cambodia,
the massacres in Rwanda.
Several years ago,
in your own time,
two teenage boys
made a videotape.
On it they chanted,
"Go, Romans, go!
Go, Romans go!
Thank God they killed that [bleeped] (meaning, Jesus).
Go, Romans, go!"[88]
One month later,
these same boys

were responsible
for killing 12 of their
fellow students
and one teacher
and wounding
several others
at Columbine High School.
This struggle here on earth
is not just against man
but against the forces of evil in the universe,
the forces of evil active here on this dark planet.[89]

One morning,
nearly 21 centuries ago,
Roman guards
came to my cell,
stripped off my clothing,
bound me,
and led me away
to be beaten and beheaded.

As a young man,
I had participated in the stoning of Stephen.
Now
I shared a similar fate.
The crushing weight
of my obligation to God,
along with the inner pressure
of self-accusation for my terrible crimes,
had been too heavy a burden to bear.
But, God had lifted that burden.
Now I was at peace,
and able to ask God to forgive my executioners.
I had fought a good fight;
I had kept the faith.[90]
And I knew

that nothing could separate me from God's love—
neither death nor life,
neither angels nor demons,
neither the present nor the future,
nor any powers,
neither height nor depth,
nor anything else in all the universe![91]
God revealed His love through His Son Jesus,
through whom He created everything
in heaven and on earth.
He made the things we can see
and the things we cannot see.
Kings, kingdoms,
rulers, and authorities—
everything has been created through Him
and for Him.
And He holds the entire universe together.[92]

Is this all so hard to believe?
How can I be sure? you ask.
Can I dare hope this is all true?
Hope in God is assured.
You can believe
because your hope does not depend on what you do.
Your hope depends on God.[93]
So do not depend on either the wisdom
or rulers of this age to guide you.
These rulers are often foolish,
disobedient,
deceived,
and enslaved
by all kinds of passion and pleasure,
living in envy and malice,
being hated,
and hating one another.[94]
When I was a young man

I was foolish,
disobedient, and
deceived.
I boasted proudly.
I acted hatefully.
But
when I became older,
I could see more clearly,
I could trust more fully,[95]
I could understand more completely.
Zeal in following the law,
violence to enforce the law,
are not God's way
but rather His Spirit of love
in our heart.[96]
Love satisfies all God's commandments.[97]
Love does no wrong to anyone.
Love is patient.
Love is kind.
It does not envy.
It does not boast.
It is not proud.
It is not rude.
It is not self-seeking.
It is not easily angered.
It keeps no record of wrongs.
Love does not delight in evil,
but rejoices in truth.
It always protects,
always trusts,
always hopes,
always perseveres.[98]

You are part of a larger story
being played out in the universe.
A great worldwide crisis is looming in the future,

and fierce suffering and convulsions will come.[99]
No one knows when this will happen—
no one but God.[100]
At that appointed time
God will send Jesus
to intervene against evil,
to save the earth and all creation.

So remember that
God has not given you
a spirit of timidity
but rather a spirit of power,
of love,
of self-discipline.[101]
Stand firm in the faith;
be of great courage.[102]
Choose truth, hope, love, and life.
Do not be afraid.
Do everything in love.[103]

Amen.

Chapter 8

The Disciple John
A New Heaven – A New Earth

When I saw him, I fell at his feet as though dead. Then he placed his right hand on me and said, "Do not be afraid. I am the First and the Last. I am the Living One; I was dead, and behold I am alive for ever and ever! And I hold the keys of death and Hades. Write, therefore, what you have seen, what is now and what will take place later" (Revelation 1:17-19 NIV).

───

The one true God of the Universe,
The Alpha and the Omega,
The First and the Last,
the Beginning and the End,[1]
has sent me to you.

My name is John.
I am a descendant of Abraham,
one of God's chosen people,
led out of bondage from Egypt
by Moses
to receive the Law
and to be a light to the world for God.
Two thousand years ago,
as a young man in Galilee,
I was expecting the Messiah to come
to free us from the evil of Rome.

I met Jesus of Nazareth,
and became one of His disciples.
Jesus was a faithful and true witness to God[2]
but he was ridiculed and rejected
at the cost of His life.
I know this to be true[3]
because I was there.
I am an eyewitness.
I watched Him die on the cross.[4]

Ten days later
I saw that same Jesus,
raised from the dead,
confront and forgive Thomas.[5]

I knew that murderer, Saul of Tarsus.
I knew that same man,
later known as Paul,
the last human to see the resurrected Jesus.

Near the end of my life
God revealed to me
His purpose for human history.[6]
In visions I was taken to God's throne room
where I saw the events on earth
from God's perspective
and was told to write them down.[7]

Before I begin
to tell my story,
please join me in prayer.

"Rise Up"

God on High,
Hear this prayer.

In our time of need
You have always been there.

Your enemies mock us.
They call us fools.
Still we believe
And trust in You.

Rise up, Oh God!
Defend Your cause.
Destroy all evil.
Restore Your laws.

Take away our pain.
May we climb upon your wings.
Wipe away our tears.
Make our spirits sing.

Amen

I have been sent to tell you
what has happened,
what is happening,
and what is going to happen.[8]

Today,
many of you
believe that mankind
is on the leading edge
of human development
with scientific and economic advancements,
democratic freedom,
and wider education.
You believe the world is made up of good people
and is progressing to a better,
fuller, more perfect end.[9]

Nevertheless,
things are happening in ways you don't understand
and don't like.
It all feels worse at the basic level
of what's right and what's wrong. [10]
There is foreboding about the future;
you feel it in your bones.
Something is wrong. [11]

God has asked of you
three things:
to have no other Gods before Him, [12]
to love one another, [13]
and to take care of His creation,
Earth. [14]

In the past one hundred years
Earth has begun shuddering
under your constantly expanding demands of her,
collapsing her fisheries,
harvesting her forests,
depleting her water tables. [15]
The evil behind the rulers of earth
has developed a global economy,
driven by greed, that is ravaging earth's resources.
Between eighty-five and ninety percent
of the wealth in the world
is controlled
by ten percent of the population. [16]
At the present rate,
you are destroying other living species on earth
at ten thousand times the normal rate. [17]
Something is wrong.

Where is love?
The past one hundred years

have been the most bestial in recorded history.[18]
The rulers of earth
have brought about wars
accounting for thirty-five million military
and fifty-four million civilian deaths.[19]
Through systematic government-sponsored genocide,
gas chambers,
mass slaying,
and policy decisions that bring on famine,[20]
the rulers of earth have murdered
over one hundred million people.[21]
Each year
nine million people,
mostly children,
die of starvation.[22]
Something is wrong.

Thirty-five hundred years ago
the Egyptians worshiped thousands of different gods.
Two thousand years ago
Romans worshiped Caesar as God.
About one hundred years ago
humans began to proudly boast,
"There is no God!
Science is advancing.
Earth is no special place. History is not progressive.
God is dead."[23]

You might be asking,
Where is this all-powerful God,
while all the death and suffering
are happening in the world?
You turned away from God.
Now you raise your fist in anger
and question the God you turned away from.
God seems to be absent

because evil is here in this world.[24]
But His Holy Spirit is present,
working on earth through the family of God.
God did not abolish humans and evil
when they rejected Him
but rather chose to allow all creation to see
the consequences
of this rejection and separation from His love.[25]
What God has done,
is doing,
and will do about evil
is unfolding over thousands of years.
He has grieved over death and suffering
and has taken them upon Himself,
having begun
to rid creation of the ancient evil.[26]
I know this
because I was there
two thousand years ago
when it began.

I sat next to Jesus at our last supper
the night before He died.
Afterward
He went off to pray.
I heard His agony.

He asked God that He not be crucified.[27]
But God withdrew.
At a cost of tremendous personal pain
God did not answer His son's prayer.
Forsaken,
Jesus had to stand on His own.
Without God's help,
Jesus offered His free obedience,
sacrificing Himself to crucifixion for mankind.

All creation watched in horror
as He was beaten and crucified by humans on earth.

Jesus was seized,
tried by the Jewish leaders,
taken to Pontius Pilate,
then to Herod,
then back to Pilate,
who ordered Him scourged.[28]
Most of the followers of Jesus were in hiding,
but Mary and a few of the women
came into Jerusalem and met me.
We found Jesus,
being led by Roman soldiers
into a small courtyard.
At the center
were three stone pillars about three feet tall.[29]
The soldiers grabbed Jesus,
stripped Him,
and shoved Him over one of the pillars,
securing His hands in two iron rings at the base.
Out strode a strong,
arrogant young man,
grinning broadly.
He grabbed a flagellum,
a piece of wood with leather straps
that had ragged bone chips sewn on the ends.[30]

He bent over,
glaring at Jesus
with contempt.
He stood up abruptly,
knocked Jesus' legs apart,
stepped back,
and snapped the flagellum,
splitting the air with a sharp blistering crack.

A chill of terror swept through me.
Mary was gripping my arm with all her strength.

The evil behind Rome
rocked back,
extending his whip all the way—paused—then,
whistled it through the air at full strength.
The leather and bone chips
tore into the back of Jesus.
Gleefully,
with a fierce hatred,
the young man picked up the pace
with a slow steady rhythm,
each searing stroke,
repeated again and again and again.
It lasted about three minutes.[31]
When it was over,
the soldiers grabbed Jesus by the arms
and lifted Him up.
His hair was disheveled,
matted with blood,
eyes sunken,
face ravaged with pain.

With a surge of relief
I thought to myself,
at least it was over.
Back to Pilate,
then Jesus would be released.
We would carry Him back to Bethany
and nurse Him back to health.

But, the worst was yet to come.
When Jesus went back before Pilate,
the crowd,
in a wave of hate and fury,

started chanting,
"CRUCIFY HIM! CRUCIFY HIM!"[32]

I felt hopeless
against this onslaught of hatred.
To my horror
Pilate agreed.
The crowd cheered.
Jesus was to be crucified!
Panic engulfed me.
Mary was sobbing,
her eyes red and swollen from crying.

The hands of Jesus were tied,
and a thirty-pound crossbeam placed on His right shoulder.
Roman soldiers prodded Him
to begin walking up a narrow incline
to Gennath Gate.
Jesus collapsed.
The crowd,
on rooftops,
looking out windows,
cursed and jeered Him.
At Golgotha
the Roman soldiers stripped Jesus,
wrapped a cloth around His loins,
then yanked Him backward.
His head hit the cross beam.
Soldiers sat on His chest
to hold Him down.[33]
The executioner,
teeth bared,
nostrils distended,
eyes bulging,
pulled out two five-inch nails from his apron.
He probed the wrist of Jesus,

looking for the small hollow spot.
Then—
coldly,
calculatingly,
and ruthlessly,
he drove the nails into one wrist,
then the other.

When he was sure
that Jesus could not pull Himself loose,
he signaled for the cross to be lifted
and dropped in its hole.
Jesus sagged on His wrists
making a "V,"
hanging from two nails.
Roman soldiers lifted his right foot over his left
and pushed his feet up the cross.
The ancient evil
placed a five-inch nail over His right foot.
Then,
with a satisfying hate,
drove the final nail through His feet.
Jesus was crucified.

My whole body was electrified with fear.
I couldn't talk.
I couldn't think.
I was numb.
They were not fatal wounds
but the agony was extreme.
As Jesus breathed in,
He had to raise Himself on His feet to exhale.
His muscles started to cramp
and then slow, steady pain intensified.[34]
He was shaking all over,[35]
jaw clenched,

lips trembling.
I could not look.
The crowd shouted at Him,
taunting Him
with savage sarcasm.[36]

I stayed to the end.
Jesus struggled on the cross
for three hours.[37]
In all His pain,
He did not curse them
or revile them,
but asked God to forgive them.[38]

No one has suffered more unjustly from evil
than God and His Son.
Then,
it was over.
The ancient evil had won.
Death triumphed.
There was no hope.

But, three days later
something shocking,
something totally unexpected
happened.
There was hope.
God intervened in our world.
Heaven and earth intersected and interlocked.
God raised Jesus
from the dead.[39]
Jesus appeared to us,
His disciples,
several times,
as normal
but radically transformed.

He would suddenly appear and then disappear,
teaching and helping us to understand
what had happened.[40]
After forty days, He ascended into God's space
in heaven.[41]

Seventy years later
our numbers had grown,
but as followers of Jesus,
we were being attacked on all sides.
The teachings of Jesus
were being diluted
and misrepresented.
False prophets,
claiming to be apostles,
were leading many astray.[42]

Mary,
the mother of Jesus,
had left us.
Lazarus had died.
Peter had been crucified,
Paul beheaded,
and all the other disciples martyred.[43]
I was one of the last remaining eyewitnesses.

When He was with us,
we asked Jesus
how to pray.[44]
He told us God His father
was open to meet humans
and partner with us through prayer,[45]
but our prayers were half-hearted and weak.
He taught us to pray
the most powerful request
we could ask of God.

That God's kingdom of heaven
would come to Earth,
that God would deliver us from evil,
and that God's will would be done
on Earth
as it is in heaven.[46]
Despite all my prayers,
God's kingdom had not come to Earth.
Evil continued to flourish,
and the righteous continued to suffer.
I was puzzled and confused.
He did not answer.
He did not come.
My faith tested by unanswered prayers,
I had waited and waited,
but Jesus had not returned.

Now,
I was over ninety,
my body broken down,
living on the Isle of Patmos.[47]
The grief,
the unfulfilled dreams,
the losses and hurt over the years
had taken their toll.

The dull ache and pain
of loneliness
wore on me daily.
I wanted to give up.
It seemed hopeless,
but hope is not cheap,
for hope that is seen
is not hope at all.[48]
I did not give up.
I did not quit.

I kept the faith
and remained certain of what I could not see.[49]

Then, one day
I heard a voice behind me
like a thundering waterfall.
I turned around
and saw a man in a long robe
with a golden sash,
eyes blazing,
face shining like the sun.[50]
I gasped for breath
and fell down as though dead.
He placed His hand on my shoulder.
I felt a surge of power,
love,
and pure joy.
He told me not to be afraid
and that I was to write down
what I had seen,
what is now,
and what is going to happen.[51]
I was taken outside of time
to God's kingdom in heaven,
to His throne room.
What I saw—
and what I wrote down—
is the most prophetic,
most controversial,
and most misunderstood
book of human history.
This is what I saw.

I saw a scroll with writing on it,
and a mighty voice called out,
"Who is worthy to open the scroll?"

No one in heaven,
or on earth,[52]
except one.

I saw Jesus, the one
I had watched being crucified
for all the evil in the universe,
come forward.
He was worthy.
The scroll was opened,
and a series of increasingly severe warnings,
designed to turn humans back to God,
were released.
But like Pharaoh,
thousands of years before,
many human hearts were hardened and
those warnings did not turn all men back to God.[53]

I saw believers,
crying out for justice,[54]
pleading with God
to act against evil on Earth.
But they were told they must wait
because of God's patience and unrelenting love,
not wanting any human to perish
but for many to come to repentance.[55]
And I saw faithful believers still on earth,
actively participating
in a struggle to the death against evil.
They were witnessing to the world,
having courage,
spreading the word about God's truth,
fighting injustice,
acting in love,
feeding the hungry,
healing the sick,

sheltering the homeless,
rescuing the oppressed,
protecting the earth,
rejecting the lie.
They were prepared to die.[56]
Those witnesses,
through sacrifice and love,
led many to genuine repentance
and acknowledgement of the one true God.

Because of the ancient evil's intense hatred for God,
he would not tolerate those faithful witnesses.
Earth's rulers,
opposing God's kingdom on earth,[57]
used extreme violence to stop believers.
It was a time of fierce suffering and convulsions;[58]
those faithful witnesses were persecuted.
And the world gloated and celebrated over their deaths.

The severity of the warnings increased.
The anxiety
reduced the world
to a nightmare of complete chaos.
Humans,
who are the pinnacle of God's creation,
the center of His affection,
and given responsibility for taking care of His Earth,
cursed God.[59]
The rulers of earth
had amassed thousands of chemical,
biological,
and nuclear weapons.
Their sheer political and military power
seemed overwhelming.[60]
The rulers of Earth
started to war

over the depleted resources of the Earth.
The evil,
indwelt in humans,
was bringing
unimaginable
death and suffering into the world,
threatening the very existence of the planet.
It seemed hopeless,
but there was one hope.

What God was going to do next
for His creation
and for all those who love Him,
no ear could hear,
no eye could see,
no mind could conceive.[61]
It was the beginning
of the consummation of human history.

God's tolerance for the evil
that was destroying His good creation
ended.
I saw God intervene.
The kingdom of heaven was no longer hidden,
but revealed and seen by all.
Jesus appeared
and God's truth was made known to all.[62]
The lies of economic and military rulers of the world
were exposed and destroyed.[63]

Ancient evil at its deepest level
was destroyed,
and all evil and death were vanquished from creation.[64]
Now all that had ever happened
was fully disclosed,
unveiling the truth.[65]

Jesus
searched the hearts and examined the minds of all,
exposing those who had turned away from the one true God.[66]
Because they had rejected God
and had no interest in seeking God,
they would not reach their full potential
as intended by their Creator.
For them all hope of a relationship with God
was lost and final.[67]

All the damage that had been done by evil
was radically healed.
Creation was restored and renewed.
I heard a loud voice proclaim,
"Now the dwelling place of God is with men,
And He will live with them."[68]
I saw a New Heaven and a New Earth.[69]

Humans were unveiled
and could again be face to face with God.
God recognized
all the faces of those who had sought after Him.
He did not turn His face away
from those who had loved Him.
For God does not love you
because you are valuable;
you are valuable
because He loves you.[70]

The faithful were united with,
accepted,
and bathed in God's love.
How can this be?
Can educated, reasonable people believe this is really going to
happen?
Two thousand years ago

I saw Jesus die on a cross.
Three days later,
Jesus suddenly and inexplicably appeared.
Without question,
it was Jesus.
He had the scars on His hands.
He ate fish.
He was not a ghost.
But it was also obvious that,
without question,
He did not belong to this world.[71]
He was transformed,
imperishable.
All of my preconceived notions about reality were destroyed.
My world was turned upside down and inside out.
It was no easier for me to accept the new reality
of the resurrected Jesus
than it is for you
to accept the new reality that
there will be a New Heaven and a New Earth
and that Jesus is truly coming again.
Accepting this reality
changes everything.

When God intervened at the Red Sea,
it changed everything for Israel.
When God appeared ten days after He was crucified,
it changed everything for Thomas.
When God confronted Paul on the road to Damascus,
it changed everything for him.
When God raised Jesus from the dead,
it changed everything for me.
When God becomes part of your life,
it will change everything for you.
And when that day comes in the future,
when God again intervenes in human history,

it will change everything
for everyone
forever.

For God's story
is *not* mere fiction,
designed to help you get through
the troubles of life.
God's story
is an enchanted,
mysterious,
grown-up
true story[72]
with a beginning, a middle, and an end.[73]
It is about good versus evil,
hope versus despair,
truth versus lies,
love versus hate.
It is all about faith and hope
in things unseen, for
faith and hope in things that are seen
is not faith at all.[74]
But this takes great strength and courage,
for you cannot say to God,
"Show me and I will believe."
But first you must believe in your heart
and confess with your mouth.
Then God will show Himself to you.
Believing or not believing God's story
is a matter of choosing eternal life or death.

Is there life after death?
What is more difficult,
to be born the first time
or reborn the second?[75]
God's larger purpose for humans is

that they love Him and love one another,
to fulfill His promise to Abraham,
to bless all the people on Earth,[76]
and do the difficult and dangerous work
of ridding His good creation of evil.

For the God of hope
so loves His creation,
the Earth,
and you,
that He gave His Son,
Jesus Christ,
that whoever believes in Him
will not perish[77]
but be given a new, imperishable
resurrected body
and join Him
on the New Earth
forever and ever and ever.

Glory to the Father,
Glory to the Son,
And to Thee, blest Spirit,
While all ages run.[78]

Now the story's over.
Now the plan is done.
Now the new beginning,
eternity has begun.

Hallelujah!

Then the angel showed me
the river of the water of life,
as clear as crystal,
flowing from the throne of God

and of the Lamb
down the middle of the great street of the city.
On each side of the river
stood the tree of life,
bearing twelve crops of fruit,
yielding its fruit every month.
And the leaves of the tree
are for the healing of the nations.
No longer will there be any curse.
The throne of God and of the Lamb
will be in the city,
And his servants will serve him.
They will see his face,
and his name will be on their foreheads.
There will be no more night.
They will not need the light of a lamp
or the light of the sun,
for the Lord God will give them light.
And they will reign for ever and ever.
The angel said to me,
"These words are trustworthy and true.
"The Lord, the God of the spirits of the prophets,
sent his angel to show his servants
the things that must soon take place…"
He who testifies to these things says,
"Yes, I am coming soon." [79]

Amen. Come, Lord Jesus.

Part III

YOUR STORY:
GOD'S PLAN FOR YOUR LIFE

Chapter 9

Prayer

My son Blair works for a non-profit organization called Amor Ministries in San Diego, California. Each year Amor guides more than twenty thousand people into Baja, Sonora, and Chihuahua, Mexico, to build more than one thousand homes and churches.

For the last seven years our family has taken Martin Luther King weekend in January to go to Mexico to build a home. The weather is usually ideal, 70 degrees in the day and 50 degrees at night.

Two thousand seven was a year to remember. As always, I prayed for a safe and successful weekend. My daughter Emily was driving over from the University of Arizona with three of her sorority sisters. My son Trevor was flying in from New York City, my son Greer from Washington D.C. My son Spencer was bringing friends from work. A total of fourteen people were on the trip.

We were to build a new Sunday school next to a church. It would be a big job, bigger than normal for our group. The Sunday school was to be two buildings built together, twice as much roof, twice as much stucco, and twice as much hammering and sawing. Because of the size of the job some of the Amor staff volunteered to help us.

We crossed the border into Mexico early Saturday morning and arrived at the site about 9:30 a.m. It was bitterly cold with a strong, biting wind. The cold was totally unexpected. We had brought all the wrong clothes. I began to worry about the trip turning out badly and no one coming back the next year.

I muttered under my breath, complaining to God about the cold. We put on all the clothes we could and tried to find some shelter inside the church. There was no relief from the penetrating old. The nails broke, the saws wouldn't cut, and our hands were too numb to work. A dread settled over me, as I realized that weekend

111

was going to be very hard. I prayed silently, asking God to give us some relief. Instead, it started to snow.

At the end of the day, wet and cold, we returned to our campsite. The tents were up and the sleeping bags all laid out. Normally, after dinner, we would all sit around the campfire, keep warm, and tell stories into the night, but not that night. A stiff cold wind swirled around the fire, blowing soot and smoke in all directions. Our eyes watered and we couldn't breathe. We couldn't get warm and were all driven to our tents and sleeping bags to escape the cold.

My wife Cynthia and I slept in our clothes, taking off our shoes when we climbed into the sleeping bags together. Several hours had passed when Emily came to our tent. The girls were freezing and asked if they could sleep in the van. Others escaped to their vehicles, but there was not enough room for everyone in the cars. The rest of us had to sleep outside on the ground.

Cynthia and I lay shivering in our sleeping bags. It was miserable. I asked God to help us get through the night. My prayer was met with a cold silence. Our tent flapped continuously in the icy wind all through the night. No one slept.

Sunday morning there was a light snow and frost on the ground. My shoes were like frozen bricks. I cursed myself for not putting them inside my sleeping bag. We all stood around, stomping our feet and holding steaming cups of coffee or hot chocolate in both hands, trying to get warm. No one had much to say.

When we arrived at the building site, the Mexican congregation of about fifty was gathering for church. They were neatly dressed, oblivious to the cold, and seemed quite happy and excited about the new Sunday school building. Mildly agitated, I ignored them, lowered my head, and walked by with a cold indifference, saying nothing.

That afternoon we started to put on the stucco. The stucco is mixed by hand, put on a hawk carrier, then spread on the side of the building with a trowel. The stucco was wet, cold, and not sticking well. It splattered all over my arms, face, and clothes. The work was dirty and messy. My arms and shoulders ached.

I was putting stucco on the wall next to the church where there was a space of only about three feet between the two buildings. It was a tight fit and I was by myself. Tired and cold, I stopped to take a break.

I heard a woman's voice. She was speaking in Spanish, loudly complaining to someone about something. I can't speak Spanish, but I could tell she was upset. I looked around. The voice was coming from inside the church. I peeked in the window. It was an old Mexican woman, wearing a long heavy coat with a scarf wrapped around her head. Her rough, weathered hands were clenched tightly in a fist. She was in front of the church, before the altar, on her knees, praying.

Embarrassed, I stepped back. I didn't want to intrude on such a private moment, but I could not look away. I watched silently. Seeing someone on her knees praying to God is a sobering experience. I wondered, *What was wrong? Did she need food? Did she need money? Was a son, daughter, or grandchild sick?* I was moved by her insistent passion. How could God not answer her prayer? I casually offered up a prayer of my own, telling God that He should consider her request.

When I finished my prayer, I was filled with uneasiness, almost an anger that seemed to grip me. Questions arose from deep inside me. *Who are you to approach God on behalf of this old woman? You know nothing of this woman or what is wrong. Who are you to darken God's council with words without knowledge?*[1]

I braced myself. *Why am I, Senior Vice-President of Toyota Motor Sales, USA, spending my valuable time in Mexico on a mission of goodwill? I am cold!*

I told myself, *Next weekend you will be back in Southern California in your million-dollar home, sitting in your easy chair in front of your big screen plasma TV with a can of beer, watching the NFL playoffs. Next weekend this old woman will still be here praying, pleading, and struggling to survive. And you…you will be safe, warm, still complaining and whining.*

So answer, Why should God be with you? Who are you to ask anything of God?

But, I was not praying for myself. I was praying for her. Would not this prayer be in harmony with God's desires? Surely, her request should be honored. How could God turn away from her?

An Amor staff member approached with a hawk carrier of fresh stucco.

"Can you speak Spanish?" I asked.

"A little," she replied.

"Can you tell me what the old woman is praying about?" I asked. She leaned forward and peeked in the window, listening intently. Suddenly, she raised her head and, smiling broadly, announced, "Oh! She's praying for us!" I was shaken.

Her prayer was answered. We finished the Sunday school building.

The old woman haunts me daily, reminding me of my arrogance and pride. Prayer is a strange thing. You might think it absurd that I pray to an invisible God about an old woman in Mexico whom I don't know and will never know. I do know that the more I pray, the more coincidences seem to happen. But traces of this invisible God in our visible world can be seen not so much by proof but by faith.

God has also answered my prayer. Our group has now grown to more than forty. As of this writing, Emily is still bringing her friends from U of A. Spencer still brings friends from work, and our son Greer brings fellow law students from Pepperdine down for the weekend. In 2010, forty-one of us built three homes. Now, when we gather around the campfire at night, telling stories, someone invariably will bring up "the year it snowed!"

There is only one fatal mistake you can make about prayer and that is to stop praying and not begin again.[2]

Maybe it's not praying as much as it is hoping. Pray every day.

Chapter 10

Trust

British Royal Historian and Knight of the Realm Scholar, Sir Leigh Teabing, leaned forward and softly explained to Sophie Neveu, "The Bible is a product of man, my dear. Not of God. The Bible did not fall magically from the clouds. Man created it as a record of tumultuous times, and it has evolved through countless translations, additions, and revisions. History has never had a definitive version of the book."[1]

Millions of moviegoers and more than sixty million readers of *The DaVinci Code* heard or read those words. Is the Bible a dusty old rulebook, created by man, that has no relevance for today? Or is the Bible inspired by God? Can you trust the Bible?

The Bible consists of two parts, the "Old Testament" and the "New Testament." The Old Testament came into existence over a period of a thousand years and includes 39 books. The New Testament came into existence within less than one hundred years after Jesus and includes 27 books. The Bible is a vital and central element in belief in God.[2]

Can you trust that the Bible is historically accurate? Consider other ancient authors and their works. Plato and Homer are all recognized by scholars for their writings. Plato lived in the early 400s B.C. There are seven copies of manuscripts dated approximately 1,200 years after his death.[3] Homer's *Iliad* is believed to have been written in 850 B.C. with its earliest copy dated A.D. 300, again with a gap of more than 1,000 years.[4]

Flavius Josephus was a Roman historian who lived from A.D. 37 to A.D. 100. His writings are more than 1,900 years old, and are considered a factual source of information about his times. Josephus wrote about the Jewish Scriptures, "For although such long ages have passed, no Jew has ventured to add, or to remove, or to alter a syllable, and it is an instinct for every Jew, from the day of his birth, to regard these decrees of God, to abide by them, and if need be, die by them."[5]

Up until 1947, the oldest copy of the Old Testament was dated A. D. 980. But with the discovery of the Dead Sea Scrolls in Qumran that are dated 250 B.C., the gap of 1,000 years was closed. The text of the Dead Sea Scrolls is 95 percent identical to the manuscript dated A. D. 980. The remaining 5 percent are mainly spelling variations.[6]

The New Testament is in a league of its own in comparison with other writings of antiquity. There are more than 5,000 New Testament manuscripts categorized in many different languages, Greek, Latin, Syriac, Coptic. The oldest copies were written within one hundred years of the events by eyewitnesses or people who knew the eyewitnesses. The manuscripts maintain accuracy to 99.5 percent. The quantity and accuracy of the New Testament writings are overwhelming when compared to other writings of antiquity.[7]

Josephus, in *The Antiquities of the Jews*, acknowledges the existence of Jesus and records events consistent with the New Testament writings. The Roman historian Tacitus, in *Annals of Imperial Rome*, written in A.D. 116, records the vicious persecutions of Christians by Nero in A.D. 64 after Rome burned.[8] Scholars trust the accuracy of Plato, Homer, Josephus, and Tacitus, and you can trust the accuracy of the Bible.

Is the Bible inspired by God? When you read the Bible, you expect God's Word to be straightforward and clear, but you find it both simple and complex. You find a long list of tribes. You look again and read about prophets with strange names, about people with big ideas who make big mistakes. You find stories of murder, adultery, and greed, but also stories about courage, sacrifice, and love. The Bible hides nothing. All the arguments against God and complaints about Him are in the Bible and so are the answers, although not always easy to find or accept.[9]

The apostle Paul wrote to Timothy that the Bible is inspired by God. Paul did not say it was dictated by God, nor did he say God wrote it. The Bible is one of those points where heaven and earth intersect. It doesn't mean we can see everything at once, but it does enable us to understand better. The Bible is a true mystery, as its answers raise more questions because of the broad and infinite nature of God.[10]

Futurists try to predict events and changing trends of the coming years. If you study all the predictions made by futurists 100 years ago, you will not find anyone who has been accurate.

But the Bible has a powerful track record. More Bibles have been printed than any other book in history. More than five billion since 1815 have been translated into two thousand different languages.[11] The Bible was written over a period of one thousand years by writers, compilers, and editors of different personalities, styles, methods, and intentions, who were caught up in the strange purpose of God to redeem His creation from evil.[12]

Nevertheless, unlike futurists, the Bible's message is consistent and unchanging. The Bible is timeless in that it has a vision of God that has not ever changed. It tells us we are made in God's image, that we are part of God's plan, that God has shown His love for us by submitting to crucifixion on the cross, that He has defeated death and will redeem His creation. Nothing has changed; nothing at all.[13]

Psalm 111 in the Old Testament states, "The fear of the Lord is the beginning of wisdom." Paul writes in First Corinthians that the foolishness of God is wiser than the wisest of men.

If the learned, but fictional, Sir Leigh Teabing was to read one book for each day of his adult life, he could read 18,250 books. There are more than thirty million books in the Library of Congress, so Teabing would have read only six-thousandths of 1 percent of those thirty million books during his lifetime. Teabing's easy know-nothing contempt for things he rejects and knows almost nothing about is arrogance beyond belief. It is not important how much you know and read. It is important what you know and read. Could it be Sir Leigh Teabing is wrong?

Should you trust the fictional Teabing, who dismisses the Bible as not from God, or should you trust the Bible? More important than what men say is what the Bible says about God, His plan, and how you can know Him. Read expectantly from the apostle Paul's letter to the Romans as recorded in the *New Living Translation* of the Bible, for God has something He wants to say to you.

> *For the truth about God is known…instinctively…From the time the world was created, people have seen the earth and the sky and all that God made. They can clearly see His invisible qualities—His eternal power and divine nature. So they have no excuse whatsoever for not knowing God* (Romans 1:19-20).

> *All creation anticipates the day when it will join God's children in glorious freedom from death and decay. For we know that all creation has been groaning as in the pains of childbirth up to the present time* (Romans 8:21-22).

> *Has God failed to fulfill his promise to the Jews? No, for not everyone born into a Jewish family is truly a Jew! It is the children of the promise who are considered to be Abraham's children* (Romans 9:6, 8).

> *What can we say? Was God being unfair? Of course not!* (Romans 9:14).

> *Receiving God's promise is not up to us. We can't get it by choosing it or working hard for it. God will show mercy to anyone he chooses* (Romans 9:16).

> *Well then, you might say, why does God blame people for not listening? Haven't they simply done what he made them do? No, don't say that. Who are you, a mere human being, to criticize God?* (Romans 9:19-20).

> *God has every right to exercise his judgment and his power but he also has the right to be very patient with those who are the object of his judgment and fit only for destruction* (Romans 9:22).

> *Well then, what shall we say about these things? Just this: The Gentiles have been made right with God by faith, even though*

they were not seeking him. But the Jews, who tried so hard to get right with God by keeping the law, never succeeded. Why not? Because they were trying to get right with God by keeping the law and being good instead of depending on faith (Romans 9:30-32).

Abraham believed God, so God declared him to be righteous. People are declared righteous because of their faith, not because of their work (Romans 4:3, 5).

So that's why faith is the key! God's promise is given to us as a free gift (Romans 4:16).

For Christ has accomplished the whole purpose of the law. All who believe in him are made right with God (Romans 10:4).

Therefore, since we have been right in God's sight by faith, we have peace with God because of what Jesus Christ our Lord has done for us (Romans 5:1).

For if you confess with your mouth that Jesus is Lord and believe in your heart that God raised him from the dead, you will be saved. For it is by believing in your heart that you are made right with God and it is by confessing with your mouth that you are saved (Romans 10:9-10).

And we all can be saved in this same way, no matter who we are or what we have done (Romans 3:22).

And so…I plead with you to give your bodies to God. Let them be a living and holy sacrifice—the kind he will accept. When you think of what he has done for you, is this too much to ask? Don't copy the behavior and customs of this world, but let God transform you into a new person by changing the way you think (Romans 12:1-2).

Remember, each one of us will stand personally before the judgment seat of God. Yes, each of us will have to give a personal account to God (Romans 14:10, 12).

So I pray that God, who gives you hope, will keep you happy and full of peace as you believe in him. May you overflow with hope through the power of the Holy Spirit (Romans 15:13).

The Bible is here to reveal God to humans to enable us to do God's work in God's world.[14] You can trust the Bible because it is accurate, inspired by God, and has a powerful track record over thousands of years. Read the Bible.

Chapter 11
All Nations – All Peoples

The church is the community of believers promised by Jesus in the New Testament, a fulfillment of the promise to Abraham by God that through his seed, all nations and all peoples would be blessed.

The church exists for three reasons. First, to worship God. Second, to tell the people of the world about God. Tragically, the history of the church is littered with abuses. While some people have made mistakes, others in the church have made significant and courageous efforts to advance God's kingdom on earth. The list would include William Wilberforce, who brought about the end of the slave trade; Mother Teresa, who worked in the slums of Calcutta; Dietrich Bonhoffer, who opposed Hitler in Nazi Germany; Desmond Tutu and Nelson Mandela who brought an end to apartheid in South Africa; and Dr. Martin Luther King, Jr., who fought discrimination in America. Many others in the church, of course, have done considerable good to make the world a better place.

But the church also exists for a third important reason. God does not always offer believers protection from the shattering personal tragedies of life, but through fellow believers in the church He provides a maximum of support to meet these tragedies.

A seventeen-year-old girl from a good family was beautiful, healthy, vibrant, and went to church every Sunday. She had just graduated from high school, was captain of the lacrosse team, a member of the honor society, and planned to attend Western Maryland College in the fall. She had her whole life before her, when tragedy struck.

On a hot and muggy afternoon in July, she ran out to the end of a pier and dived into the Chesapeake Bay. As she lay on the bottom of the bay, she thought she was caught in a fishing net. She struggled to free herself, but couldn't and started to panic. She was running out of air! Her sister ran to her and pulled her up out of the water. Gratefully she gulped in huge amounts of air but when her sister let go she tumbled back into the water. Her sister grabbed her and started yelling wildly in near hysteria for someone to call an ambulance.

As she lay in the emergency room, she desperately tried to move her numb and motionless arms and legs. Angry and frustrated, she begged to be told what was going on. No one would say anything. A nurse entered the room and started cutting off her bathing suit, leaving her totally exposed. She silently screamed to be covered. The nurse, with casual indifference, threw a sheet over her. Humiliated and embarrassed, tears started streaming down her face, but she couldn't brush them away. No one seemed to notice she was choking on her own tears.

She could hear the nurses whispering. They were going to prepare the operating room, but had to wait for her parents before operating. Where were her parents? What was happening to her? Out of the corner of her eye she could see someone with electric hair clippers. She sobbed as she watched clumps of her blond hair fall around her head. Then she heard the sound of a high-speed drill. Sheer terror engulfed her! "No, dear God, don't let them do this to me!" she pleaded. Someone grabbed her head and started drilling into her skull.

She drifted in and out of consciousness for several days. Her friends and family talked bravely about how well she was doing, but a sense of doom hung in the air. The operation had been a success but what did that mean? When could she go home? When would the therapy start so she could walk again? No one seemed to want to say until the doctor reluctantly told them that her neck had been broken between the 4th and 5th cervical level. She was paralyzed from the shoulder down, a quadriplegic. She would never walk again or have the use of her hands.

Her parents were living in slow misery. She would not be going to college in the fall. The family finances were being stretched to the limit as her medical bills mounted. She was angry, frustrated, and utterly despondent, but she could do nothing, nothing about anything—just lie there! The endless nights were the worst, lying in a dark room, listening to the sound of suffering and agony around her, nose itching, trapped on a Stryker frame, helpless.

After several months, two friends from high school came to visit. She could hear them hesitate outside her room. As they slowly approached, one of the girls choked out, "Oh!" and the other whispered "Oh my God" They ran from the room, one sobbing while the other started vomiting in the hall.

Horror drove through her! She called out to the nurse and demanded a mirror. The nurse refused. She started yelling as loud as she could. She wanted a mirror, "NOW!" The nurse brought a mirror and slowly raised it in front of her. She looked at herself for the first time in months.

Terrified, she screamed: "OH GOD, WHAT HAVE YOU DONE TO ME?" Her eyes were bloodshot, dark, and sunken in her skull. She was nothing but a skeleton. She had lost 45 lbs, going from 125 lbs to 80 lbs. Her skin was yellow and jaundiced, head shaved and teeth black from all the medication. Life had been crushed out of her.

The nurse started sobbing, "I'm sorry. I'm sorry. I should never have shown you!" The full impact of what had happened forcefully hit her. All her dreams had been shattered. Her future seemed unendurable and endless. Staring into the lifelong bottomless pit of despair, she became suicidal, pleading with her friends to give her sleeping pills or slash her wrists. She would violently wrench her head back and forth trying to break her neck at a higher level; thereby killing herself.

She raged at the unfairness of it all. Why? Why did this happen? What kind of a God is this? What if He had wanted to prevent this accident, but couldn't? Worse yet, what if He could have stopped the accident, but didn't? Her questions were asked in anger and confusion. She learned to be wary of those people who patted her on the head and asked if it hurt. They had it all figured out with their glib and easy answers to questions about God that she had learned in her suffering were unanswerable.

The ancient evil is always stalking close by, his small voice nagging in the back of our mind, always questioning, always searching for weakness. Who is this God? What is God doing? This must be a cruel God if He will not end this poor girl's misery. Shouldn't she be allowed to die?

The apostle Paul wrote to the Romans that we live in an evil and broken world, but we should never give up. Yet, God is able to work incredible good out of unspeakable tragedy. But what possible good, you ask, could come from this life? The young girl was a useless creature, trapped in a concrete body, having to be constantly waited on to be kept alive. No good can come of this hopeless life. It's okay to let her go, to give up. It would save her family a lot of money. She should die.

It's been more than forty years since that accident, but the young girl refused to give up and die. She married a teacher, and she and Ken have been happily married for more than twenty-five years. She has received an honorary degree from Western Maryland and a total of seven honorary doctoral degrees. She has won numerous awards and commendations throughout her life. She began to draw and paint, holding the brushes with her mouth, and has successfully sold her work. She has been interviewed by Barbara Walters, appeared on the *Today Show*, and four times been on *Larry King Live*. She has authored forty-five books. She received a presidential appointment to the National Council for Disability during the time when the Americans with Disabilities Act became law. She started a non-profit company, Joni and Friends, to address the needs of the disabled. Wheels for the World has collected more than 34,000 used wheelchairs, had them rebuilt by inmates in seventeen different prisons, and distributed to the disabled around the world. She has traveled to 41 different countries, delivering wheelchairs. She has a daily five-minute radio program that is heard in more than 1,000 broadcast outlets by more than a million listeners a week.

When she was asked how it has been possible for her to accomplish so much after going through such a shattering experience, Joni Eareckson Tada said, "My church made a huge difference in my family's life as they demonstrated the love of God in practical ways." The church is a community of believers who are to encourage one another, hold one another up in faith, pray for one another, learn from and teach one another, set examples for one another to follow, and support one another to meet the tragedies of life.

We don't know and can't understand God's ways. Paul wrote the Corinthians that we can see the ways of God only in part. But the day will come when we can see fully. Until that day three things remain: faith, hope, and love. We do know that God had the honesty to take His own medicine. He died on a cross for us and made good out of an unspeakable tragedy. Maybe the cross does not answer the question of why these things happen in this broken world, but it does offer the hope that suffering and death will soon end.

The church is a community of believers from all nations and all peoples that is intended to be a light to the world, opposing the forces on earth aligned against God, keeping the faith, hoping and loving one another, fighting the good fight. Don't give up. Join a community of believers.

Chapter 12
Fear No Evil

It was A. D. 404.[1] Dawn was breaking over Rome. Amid clouds of dust, herdsmen with wild shouts and cracking whips were driving their flocks to market. The Emperor Honorius had declared a holiday. General Stilicho had defeated the Gauls. Throngs of people, clad in festive attire, hurrying about, laughing and talking, filled the streets.

Among the crowds there was a stranger from Asia, rudely clad but having an imposing presence.[2] He was a Christian monk, driven by an inner voice to come to Rome without knowing why.

For almost one thousand years Rome had occupied center stage, dominating the world. Rome's undeniable might was on display everywhere in her vast armies, her magnificent buildings, and her architecture.

Most impressive was the Colosseum. It dominated Rome. A true wonder of the world, nothing could arouse the vision of Rome's greatness more than the sight of the Colosseum. A massive structure, it rose four stories in height and had seventy-six numbered entrances through which spectators would pass. It was encrusted with marble and faced with limestone. The second and third levels were relieved with magnificent statues standing on the arches between the columns and arcades.

At the entrance to the stadium, vendors hawked their wares: cushions stuffed with leaves, programs, hats and umbrellas, cold drinks, sweet cakes, olives, and fruit. A standing-room-only crowd of more than fifty thousand was pushing and shoving its way into the Colosseum.

Inside, high above the stadium on the roof of the topmost gallery, experts were stationed to pull across the great awning to protect the crowd from the sun. The fourth and third levels were for the poorer of the population, middle class, and foreigners; this is where the stranger sat. The second level was for the lesser-distinguished Roman citizens. The arena floor was a 289 feet by 187 feet ellipse of neatly raked brown cast sand. A wall fifteen feet high surrounded the arena floor. Close to the arena floor on the first level were located the box seats for the Senate, magistrates, temple priests, and members of the emperor's family.

The Colosseum was quickly filling. Spectators were calling to one another, breaking into laughter at a witty word, and then sending it on from row to row. Army officers with glittering weapons, red-plumed helmets, and gold-inlaid sandals accepted the praise and admiration of the crowd. Members of the Senate, adorned with dazzling gems and red sandals, paraded to their seats. The stadium was filled with a sea of gaily decorated togas, white as snow. All the power, wealth, and brilliance of Rome were on display. Rome seemed everlasting, stronger than death. But the stranger knew it was not so. Rome was not stronger than death. Rome was death. The invisible, terrible presence of the ancient evil hung in the air.

A great shout of excitement arose from the crowd as the Sponsor of the Games entered the Colosseum. He carried himself with a lofty, regal demeanor, soft, yet cruel, devoted to pleasure and blood. As the sponsor, The Lord of Death was determined that these games would surpass in blood and victims anything seen before.

First on the arena floor were the cripples and dwarfs, forced to fight with wooden swords in make-believe combat. The crowd hooted with laughter but soon was bored and paid little attention to what was going on.

Suddenly, the thunderous roars of the lions pierced the air, electrifying the crowd. Below the arena floor, the trainers had been slipping pieces of human flesh to the beasts to arouse their rage and hunger. From all sides of the stadium arose an unbroken stomping and clapping, demanding blood. Not wanting to disappoint the crowd, the Lord of Death signaled for the gates to be opened.

A wretched band of prisoners stumbled out into the sun. Roman soldiers prodded them into the center of the arena. Some appeared injured, others carried small daggers, and still others were wrapped in animal skins.

The crowd quieted for a moment before letting out a great cheer as the lions slowly stalked onto the arena floor. Immense, with great shaggy heads, they gathered at one end of the arena.

In the center of the arena, the prisoners huddled together, some dropping to their knees, whimpering in anticipation of what was about to happen. The crowd, anxious for action, mocked the prisoners and shouted at the lions, urging them to feed.

A young man, his hands tied behind his back, started to run. The sudden movement startled one of the lions. Roaring mightily, the beast started to gallop and plowed into the lad, ripping and tearing with his teeth and claws. The crowd roared its approval.

Soon all the prisoners had been devoured. The crowd settled back and excitedly talked about the feeding. Pots of Arabian perfume were placed throughout the Colosseum to cover the horrible stench. Drinks mixed with honey, figs, and fruit were served.

After the intermission the crowd returned to their seats. A low buzz of anticipation filled the stadium. Next, real entertainment, men killing men. The trumpets sounded, announcing the arrival of the gladiators. Ceremoniously, they circled the arena, taking their positions. The crowd applauded.

A net fighter with a dirty face, wild hair, and dreadful smile, was standing next to a big-boned muscular prisoner. This gladiator had no armor but rather a piece of leather wrapped around his left shoulder. He had a huge net and small dagger in his left hand and a harpoon-like spear in his right.

His opponent, a prisoner, was a strong looking man with a heavy black beard and covered with hair. He had no protection and was given only a sword.

Standing erect, close by these two, a Sammite gladiator held his helmet and shield in his left hand. In his right hand was a sword he continually flipped over and over. He wore a broad leather belt around his mid-section, his right arm was wrapped in leather, and he wore armor on his right leg. He had close curled hair, bright dark eyes, and was clean shaven with noble features.

The Noble Roman eyed his opponent coldly, a young prisoner in his teens. The lad was white-skinned with yellow hair and blue eyes.

He had only a tattered shield and a small dagger. The young boy, staring blankly ahead, seemed paralyzed by fear.

Tension grew as the crowd started to clap for action. The Lord of Death signaled for the games to begin and the crowd roared.

The Noble Roman put on his helmet, dropped the visor and quickly advanced on the young lad. The boy retreated but the Noble Roman continued to press and with terrific force smashed his sword at the lad's shield, sending it flying. The crowd thumped, whistled, and cheered.

The boy started to run, tripped, and sprawled head first in the sand. The Noble Roman playfully danced around the boy, slashing at his arms and legs. The boy recoiled and huddled into a ball in the sand. The crowd laughed and ridiculed his behavior.

Weak from the loss of blood, the boy struggled to his feet. Realizing he was about to die, he braced himself and took a defensive stance, hopeless courage blazing in his eyes.

The crowd started to chant, "KILL HIM, KILL HIM—RECEIVE THE STEEL!" Louder and louder the chant grew to a crescendo. The Noble Roman acknowledged the crowd and charged the boy, stabbing him in the chest with a terrible force. A sickening crack of breaking bone cut the air as the point of the dagger sank in deep, so deep it went in to the hilt. The Noble Roman jerked at the dagger to dislodge it. The lad opened his mouth to scream but no sound came out. The stands rocked with howling!

The Colosseum was littered with twisted and broken bodies. The revolting stench of sweat, blood, and guts filled the air. The crowd was possessed. It was an unbroken thunder. It could not be satisfied except with more blood, more death.

How long will this savagery continue? How long would the ancient evil be allowed to reign? Who will have no fear and stand against this overwhelming evil?

The stranger up in the stands, full of purpose, was about to change everything. Among the sea of snow-white togas he began forcing his way through the crowd. The thundering din of the crowd began to settle into a low buzz as he reached the first row of the box seats.

He jumped down on the arena floor. Never before—never before in the history of Rome—had such a thing happened. The ancient evil was furious at the interruption.

The stranger purposely strode up to the Noble Roman and stood between him and the other gladiators keeping them apart. His voice, strong and clear, reverberated throughout the Colosseum "IN THE NAME OF CHRIST, STOP!"

The stunned crowd hooted and hollered in disbelief.

The Noble Roman began to advance.

Again the stranger called out, "IN THE NAME OF CHRIST, STOP!"

The crowd jeered and mocked the stranger. Rocks started flying from the stands.

The stranger, his arms, his legs, his whole body writhing with the wrath of God, exploded a third time, "IN THE NAME OF CHRIST, STOP!"[3]

More stones, chalices of wine, and pots were hurled out of the stands from all directions. The stranger slumped to the ground. His leathered face wore a strange light. He was beaten with unbelievable savagery by the gladiators and the rocks hurled from the stands, until he lay, an unrecognizable form on the arena floor.

An eerie silence filled the Colosseum. The crowd was spent, the sweet aroma of sacrifice drifted through the air. A haunting, mysterious melody hung in the wind that was so perfect it was hard to hear.

The ancient evil, his eyes blazing with hate, leered at the lifeless form. He heard the song. He knew the words. He knew there was a higher plan. He could not stop it as he could not stop the wind. He knew the words of the song would grow and live.

Little is known about the stranger. Those who knew him said his name was Telemachus. When the Emperor Honorius heard about what had happened that day, he declared an end to all gladiator combats in the Colosseum. Never again would gladiators fight to the death in the Colosseum. Telemachus would be the last to die on the Colosseum floor. He made a difference. He had no fear of evil.

Maybe you are not as brave as Telemachus, or have the endurance of Mother Teresa to work in the slums of Calcutta, or the grit of Desmond Tutu and Nelson Mandela to take on the apartheid in South Africa, or the courage of Dietrich Bonhoffer to take a stand against Hitler in Nazi Germany, or the leadership of Martin Luther King, Jr. to take on the discrimination in America, or the great strength of Joni Eareckson Tada, but in the 23rd Psalm of the Old Testament you are told to fear no evil.

> *The LORD is my shepherd, I shall not want.*
>> *He makes me lie down in green pastures;*
>> *He leads me beside quiet waters.*
>> *He restores my soul;*
> *He leads me in the paths of righteousness*
>> *for His name's sake.*
> *Even though I walk*
>> *through the valley of the shadow of death,*
>> *I will fear no evil,*
>> *for You are with me;*
>> *Your rod and Your staff,*
>> *they comfort me.*
> *You prepare a table before me*
>> *in the presence of my enemies;*
> *You have anointed my head with oil;*
>> *my cup overflows.*
> *Surely goodness and lovingkindness will follow me*
>> *all the days of my life,*
>> *and I will dwell in the house of the LORD*
>> *forever* (NASB).

Fighting evil forces opposed to God on earth is difficult and dangerous work, but the reward is a New Heaven and a New Earth.

N. T. Wright, former Bishop of Durham, England, explains it this way.[4] The Abbey cathedral in Durham was started in 1087 and completed almost 200 years later in 1280. A supervisor would give a stonemason a rough stone and tell him how to chisel the stone into shape and where it was to be placed in the building. The stonemason did not know what the architect was trying to accomplish or what the final outcome would look like, but, nevertheless, he did his job. After it was completed, the cathedral was—and still is—praised as one of the finest churches ever built. Any one of those stonemasons who worked on that cathedral could step back and point to the stones he had cut and be acknowledged for the part he had played in helping to make that magnificent structure.

So it is with God's New Heaven and New Earth. The apostle Paul wrote to the Corinthians that every prayer, every act of kindness, every act of love is not in vain. When the time comes and God has redeemed His creation, and we see the magnificent New Heaven and New Earth completed, we can all stand back along with Moses, Thomas, Paul, John, the old Mexican woman, the people of Amor Ministries, Ken and Joni Eareckson Tada, and Telemachus and point to the stones we cut and be acknowledged for the part we played in helping others become a part of God's new family. It will be wonderful to see how everyone contributed in his own way to made a difference

But we all have to choose to be or not to be a part of God's plan. Do you choose to believe that we are just talking animals, living without purpose, having no hope, living a life of fear that ends in death? Or, do you choose to believe we are made in the image of God, living with purpose, having hope, living a life with no fear, a life that never ends but enjoys eternal life?

Maybe it's not only a choice but also a hope.

As for me and my house, we choose hope—the God of Hope.

Endnotes

Chapter 5

1 Ephesians 3:18
2 Biblical Archaeology Society, online archive
3 Matthew 27:2
4 *Baker's Bible Atlas*, 109
5 Mark 6:22-28
6 Manning, *Abba's Child*, 81
7 Matthew 3:1-3
8 Yancey, *What's So Amazing About Grace?*, 193-198
9 Matthew 22:37-39
10 MacArthur, *Twelve Ordinary Men*, 24
11 Wright, *Jesus and the Victory of God*, 162
12 Luke 4:28-29
13 John 10:40-41
14 John 11:2
15 John 11:14-15
16 John 11:18
17 Wright, *Jesus and Victory*, 172
18 Luke 13:31
19 John 10:31-33
20 John 11:16
21 John 11:39
22 John 11:41-44
23 Luke 20:27
24 Wright, *Jesus and Victory*, 190
25 John 11:54
26 *Baker's Bible Atlas*, 206
27 John 12:10
28 John 12:17-18

29 John 11:45, 12:11
30 John 12:12-15
31 John 13:30
32 John 13:33
33 John 13:36
34 John 14:1-5
35 John 14:6-7
36 John 14:15-20, 16:7-15
37 Luke 22:45
38 John 18:3-12
39 Martin, *Hostage to the Devil*, 455
40 Matthew 26:65
41 Luke 23:6-11
42 John 19:1
43 John 19:16-18
44 Matthew 27:65-66
45 Matthew 27:3-5
46 John 20:1-4
47 John 20:10
48 John 20:18
49 John 20:22
50 John 20:24-25
51 John 20:26
52 John 20:26
53 John 20:27
54 Romans 10:10
55 John 20:28
56 Romans 5:1
57 John 20:29
58 Acts 1:15

Chapter 6

1 *Life Application Bible*, Exodus Introduction
2 Möller, *The Exodus Case*, 104
3 Exodus 6:20
4 Kirsch, *Moses: A Life*, 2

5   Kirsch, *Moses,* 15
6   Olson, *Mapping Human History,* 25-27, 106-119
7   Möller, 12
8   Fletcher, *Chronicle of a Pharaoh,* 76
9   White, *Ancient Egypt, Its Culture and History,* 1-7
10   White, 21
11   Watts, "Why Should God Care Less?" a sermon at Mt Hermon, August 2004
12   White, 6
13   Watts, "Why Should God Care Less?"
14   Oakes and Gahlin, *Ancient Egypt,* 263
15   Watts, "What Does It Mean to Be Human?" a sermon at Mt. Hermon, August 2004
16   Oakes and Gahlin, 297
17   Exodus 1:9-11
18   Kirsch, *Moses,* 33
19   Exodus 1:16
20   Kirsch, *Moses,* 37
21   Exodus 1:22
22   Exodus 2:2-3
23   Josephus, *Antiquities of the Jews,* Book 2/9:4-5
24   Exodus 2:6-10
25   Fletcher, 146-148
26   Acts 7:20-22
27   Josephus, Book 2/9:7
28   Möller, 107
29   Exodus 2:11-12
30   Exodus 2:15
31   Deuteronomy 8:2-15
32   Exodus 2:15
33   Exodus 3:1
34   Packer, *Knowing God,* 88
35   Wright, *Simply Christian,* 8
36   Colson, *The Good Life,* 8
37   Deuteronomy 4:32
38   Young, *The Shack,* 190

39   Genesis 1:28-30
40   Wright, *Evil and the Justice of God*, 109
41   Revelation 12:3-9, Luke 10:18
42   Genesis 3:1-7
43   Lewis, *Perelandra*, 119-136
44   Wright, *Evil and Justice*, 71-74
45   Tozer, *The Knowledge of the Holy*, 110
46   Polkinghorne, *Science and Theology*, 65
47   Genesis 12:2-3
48   Packer, 76
49   Exodus 3:1
50   Kirsch, *Moses*, 108
51   Wright, *Simple Christianity*, 64
52   Exodus 3:5-15
53   Exodus 4:12-17
54   Exodus 5:1
55   Exodus 5:6-9
56   Exodus 7:20-21; 8:5-6; 9:9-10, 23; 10:13, 22
57   Exodus 7:13-14; 8:15, 32; 9:34; 10:27
58   Exodus 5:21
59   Exodus 10:28
60   Exodus 12:21-23
61   Exodus 12:31
62   Josephus, Book 2, 14:6
63   Möller, 181-182
64   Exodus 13:17-18
65   Möller, 168
66   Exodus 14:5
67   Kirsch, *Moses*, 186
68   Josephus, Book 2/15:5
69   Möller, 188-190
70   Exodus 14:11-12
71   Exodus 14:13
72   Exodus 14:27-28
73   Watts, "Why Should God Care Less?"
74   Josephus, Book 2/16-5

75 Exodus 15:22
76 Regele, "The Amalekite Problem," a sermon delivered at Irvine Presbyterian Church, August 2005
77 Deuteronomy 25:17-19
78 Regele, "Amalekite Problem"
79 Exodus 17:8-13
80 Exodus 19:1
81 Exodus 32:1-6
82 Watts, "What Does It Mean to Be Human?"
83 Exodus 32:20
84 Exodus 32:31-32
85 Exodus 33:1
86 Exodus 34:27
87 Exodus 34:29-30
88 Kirsch, *Moses,* 274-275
89 Exodus 34:35
90 Kirsch, *Moses,* 277
91 Exodus 17:1-7
92 Numbers 13:1-20
93 Number 13:28-33
94 Numbers 14:1-4
95 Numbers 14:5
96 Numbers 14:34
97 Fieler, *Walking the Bible*, 297
98 Deuteronomy 8:15-16
99 Regele, "Amalekite Problem"
100 Deuteronomy 4:29
101 Deuteronomy 30:11
102 Deuteronomy 30:15-16
103 Deuteronomy 30:19
104 Deuteronomy 3:23-25
105 Deuteronomy 34:1
106 Deuteronomy 31:23
107 Wright, *Evil and Justice*, 58
108 Deuteronomy 31:27
109 Deuteronomy 31:24-27

110 Deuteronomy 31:14
111 Tozer, 84
112 Packer, 77
113 Regele, "Finally Faces," a lesson delivered at Irvine
     Presbyterian Church, 2006
114 Bauckham, *The Theology of the Book of Revelation*, 142
115 Lewis, *Weight of Glory*, 42
116 2 Corinthians 3:13-18
117 Isaiah 40:31
118 Joncas, "On Eagles Wings," Words and Music, 1971
119 Numbers 6:24-26

Chapter 7

1   Acts 22:3
2   Acts 9:1-2
3   Acts 22:4
4   Wright, "The Paul of History and the Apostle of Faith,"
    lecture
5   Wright, *New Perspective on Paul*, 4
6   Ephesians 1:9-10
7   Acts 22:3
8   Swindoll, *Paul: A Man of Grace and Grit*, 4-5
9   Sanders, *Paul: A Very Short Introduction*, 11
10 Galatians 1:14
11 Ehrman, *Peter, Paul, and Mary Magdalene*, 105
12 Wright, *Paul, Arabia, and Elijah*, 2
13 Acts 26:5
14 Romans 9:4-5
15 Wright, *The Resurrection and the Post-Modern Dilemma*, 5
16 Isaiah 34:1-8
17 Acts 3:11
18 Acts 4:32
19 Ehrman, 231
20 John 1:46
21 Acts 4:5-7
22 Acts 5:33

23 Acts 5:30

24 Acts 5:39

25 Acts 5:40

26 Ehrman, 122

27 Forbush, *Fox's Book of Martyrs*, 2

28 Acts 26:9-10

29 Acts 6:11

30 Acts 7:54-58

31 Wangerin, *Paul: A Novel*, 35-36

32 Acts 7:60

33 Sahebjam, *The Stoning of Soraya M*, 115-125

34 Acts 8:1-4

35 Acts 26:13

36 Acts 26:14

37 Acts 26:15

38 Lewis, *The Last Battle*, 204-206

39 Acts 26:16-18

40 Acts 9:9

41 Sanders, 11

42 Wright, "Two Radical Jews," 4

43 Wangerin, 70

44 1 Corinthians 15:42

45 Wright, *Creation and Covenant*, 5

46 Acts 9:17

47 Acts 9:15

48 Lewis, *The Last Battle,* 204-206

49 Ephesians 3:8

50 Acts 26:21

51 Galatians 1:17-18

52 Swindoll, 54

53 Sanders, 116-117

54 Ibid., 48

55 Genesis 3:1-7

56 Genesis 12:1-3

57 Romans 2:17-20

58 Romans 2:21-24

59 Ehrman, 21

60 Loc. cit.

61 Wright, "A New Reading of Romans," 2

62 Wright, "Paul's Gospel and Caesar's Empire," 4

63 Benario, *Roman Rulers*, 8

64 Romans 8:22

65 Wright, "New Perspectives," 4-5

66 Wright, "A New Reading of Romans," 6

67 Ephesians 1:9-11

68 Ephesians 3:14-15

69 Wright, *Paul of History*, 5

70 Wright, Ibid., 8

71 Luke 4:1-14

72 Wright, "A New Reading of Romans ,"10

73 Isaiah 53:3-12

74 Romans 9:8

75 1 Corinthians 15:21-25

76 Wright, "A New Reading of Romans*,*"8

77 1 Corinthians 15:58

78 Wright, "A New Reading of Romans, "10

79 Ephesians 6:19

80 2 Corinthians 11:23-28

81 Acts 14:19

82 Acts 23:12-13

83 Benario, 4

84 Benario, 7

85 Lewis, *A Grief Observed*, 25

86 Forbush, 4

87 Benario, 8

88 Scott et. al. *Rachel's Tears*, 90

89 Ephesians 6:12

90 2 Timothy 4:7

91 Romans 8:38-39

92 Colossians 1:15-17

93 Romans 9:16

94 Titus 3:3

95 2 Timothy 1:7
96 Wright, "Paul, Arabia…,"
97 Galatians 5:14
98 1 Corinthians 13:1-8
99 Wright, "A New Reading of Romans," 9
100 Mark 13:32
101 2 Timothy 1:7
102 2 Thessalonians 2:15; 1 Corinthians 16:13
103 1 Corinthians 16:14

Chapter 8

1 Revelation 22:13
2 Revelation 1:5
3 John 21:24
4 John 19:16-37
5 John 20:24-29
6 Bauckham, *Theology*, 7
7 Revelation 1:11
8 Revelation 1:19
9 Wright, *Evil and Justice*, 21-23
10 Strauss and Howe, *The Fourth Turning*, 3-4
11 Wright, *Simple Christianity*, 2-8
12 Exodus 20:5
13 Leviticus 19:18
14 Genesis 1:28-30
15 Brown, *Outgrowing the Earth*, 4, 8, 26
16 Hanlon, *How the World's Wealth is Distributed*, gizmag.com
17 Polkinghorne, *Science and Theology*, 132
18 Bauckham and Hart, *Hope Against Hope*, 15
19 Brzezinski, *Out of Control, Global Turmoil on the Eve of the Twenty-First Century, 1993*
20 Meredith, *The Elephant and the Dragon*, 19
21 D'Souza, *What's So Great About Christianity*, 215
22 FriendsoftheWorldFoodProgram.org
23 Neitzche, *The Gay Science*, 181-182

24 Bauckham, *Theology*, 47

25 Barnhouse, *The Invisible War*, 51

26 Wright, *Evil and Justice*, 94

27 Matthew 26:39-43

28 John 18, 19

29 Bishop, *The Day Christ Died*, 231

30 Ibid., 232

31 Ibid., 233

32 John 19:6

33 Buckley, *Nearer My God*, 131

34 Bishop, 241-250

35 Buckley, 136

36 Mark 15:29-32

37 Bishop, 256

38 Luke 23:34

39 1 Corinthians 15:3-5

40 John 20:19-21:14

41 Luke 24:51

42 Revelation 2:20

43 Forbush, 1-5

44 Luke 11:1

45 Wright, *Surprised by Hope*, 277-280

46 Matthew 6:9-13

47 Revelation 1:9

48 Romans 8:24

49 Hebrews 11:1

50 Revelation 1:12-16

51 Revelation 1:17-19

52 Revelation 5:2-3

53 Bauckham, *Theology*, 82

54 Revelation 6:9-10

55 1 Peter 3:9, Revelation 6:11

56 Bauckham, *Theology*, 86-88

57 Bauckham, *Prophecy*, 309-310

58 Wright, "A New Reading of Romans," 9

59 Revelation 16:21

60 Bauckham, *Prophecy*, 235
61 1 Corinthians 2:9
62 Revelation 19:11
63 Revelation 19:20-21
64 Revelation 20:10
65 Revelation 20:12-15
66 Romans 2:15-16
67 Bauckham and Hart, 146
68 Revelation 21:3
69 Revelation 21:2
70 Ian Pitt Watson, "A Kind of Loving," a sermon at Irvine Presbyterian Church, Nov. 1990
71 Bauckham and Hart, 104
72 Patterson, "Uses of Enchantment," a sermon at Irvine Presbyterian Church, January 1989
73 Wright, *Surprised by Hope*, 143
74 Romans 8:24
75 Pascal, *The Pensees*, 274
76 Wright, *Surprised by Hope*, 197
77 John 3:16
78 "Now the Day is Over," Words by Sabine Baring-Gould, Music by Merrial Joseph Barnby
79 Revelation 22:1-6, 20

Chapter 9

1 Job 38:1-2
2 Yancey, *Prayer,* 9

Chapter 10

1 Brown, *DaVinci Code*, 250-251
2 Wright, *Simple Christianity*, 173-174
3 Slick, "Manuscript Evidence for Superior New Testament Reliability," carm.org
4 Strobel, *The Case for Christ*, 60
5 Josephus, *Antiquities of the Jews*

6 Brantley, *The Dead Sea Scrolls and Biblical Integrity*, apologeticspress.org
7 Strobel, 45
8 Ibid., 60
9 Roberts, *Finding God in Hard Time Through the Bible*, sermon, Irvine Presbyterian Church, 2/26/06
10 Bell, *Velvet Elvis*, 32
11 Christian Biblical Church of God, "Why Are There So Many Bibles in the World?" biblestudy.org
12 Wright, *Simple Christianity*, 184
13 Buckley, *Nearer My God*, "Introduction," XIX
14 Wright, *Simple Christianity*

Chapter 12

1 Preston, *The Monk Who Ended the Colosseum Games*, prayerfoundation.org
2 Forbush, 6
3 Preston
4 Wright, lecture at St. Andrews Presbyterian Church, Newport Beach, Calif., 2008

Bibliography

"A Day In The Life Of Pharaoh." Special Feature, PBS Television, *Egypt Golden Empire*, PBS.org/empires/Egypt/special/lifeas/pharaoh.

Barnhouse, Donald Grey. *The Invisible War*. Grand Rapids: Zondervan, 1965.

Baring-Gould, Sabine, words, and Merrial Joseph Barnby, music. "Now the Day Is Over." *The Church Times,* February 1867.

Bauckham, Richard. *The Theology of the Book of Revelation*. New York: Cambridge University Press, 1993.

_____ *The Climax of Prophecy*. London: T&T Clark, 1993.

Bauckham, Richard and Trevor Hart. *Hope Against Hope*. Grand Rapids: William B. Eerdman Publishing Company, 1999.

Bell, Rob. *Velvet Elvis*. Grand Rapids: Zondervan, 2005.

Benario, Herbert W. "Nero (54-68 A.D.)". http://www.roman-emperors.org/nero.htm.

Biblical Archaeology Society, Online Archive. "Estimation of the Population of Ancient Jerusalem." http://www.basarchieve.org/bsubsearch.asp.

Bishop, Jim. *The Day Christ Died*. New York: Harper Collins, 1957.

Brantely, Garry K., "The Dead Sea Scrolls and Biblical Integrity." Apologetics Press.org, April 1995.

Brown, Dan. *The DaVinci Code*. New York:Random House Publishing, 2003.

Brown, Lester R. *Outgrowing the Earth*. New York: W.W. Norton and Company, 2004.

Bruce, A.B. *The Training of the Twelve*. Grand Rapids: Kegel Publications, 2002.

Brzezinski, Zbigniew. *Out of Control: Global Turmoil on the Eve of the Twenty-First Century*. Norwalk, Conn.: Easton Press, 1993.

Buckley, William F., Jr. *Nearer My God*. New York:Doubleday Publishing, 1997.

Colson, Charles. *The Good Life*. Wheaton, Ill.: Tyndale House Publishing, 2005.

D'Souza, Dinesh. *What's So Great About Christianity*. Washington, D. C.: Regency Publishing, 2007.

Eareckson Tada, Joni. *Joni: An Unforgettable Story*. Grand Rapids: Zondervan, 1976.

Ehrman, Burt D. *Peter, Paul, and Mary Magdalene*. New York: Oxford University Press, 2006.

Fieler, Bruce. *Walking the Bible*. New York: Harper-Collins Publishers, 2001.

Fletcher, Joann. *Chronicle of a Pharaoh*. New York: Oxford University Press, 2001.

Forbush, William Bryan. *Fox's Book of Martyrs*. Grand Rapids: Zondervan, 1967.

Friends of the World Food Program, www.friendsofwfp.org.

Hanlon, Mike. "How the World's Wealth is Distributed.: www.gizmag.com, November 6, 2006.

History of Writing. wikipedia.org/wiki/history_of_writing.

Holy Bible. New Living Translation. Wheaton, Ill.: Tyndale House Publishing, 1996.

Holy Bible. The New International Version Worship Bible. Grand Rapids: Zondervan, 2000.

"Imperial Cult (Ancient Rome)." http://en.wikipedia.org/wiki/Imperial_cult%28Ancient_ Rome%29.

Joncas, Michael. "On Eagles Wings." New Dawn Music, 1997.

Josephus, Flavius. *Antiquities of the Jews.* Interhook. met/projects/library/antiquities-jews/b3c2.

Kirsch, Jonathan. *Moses: A Life.* New York: Ballentine Books, 1998.

_____ *A History of the End of the World.* New York: Harper-Collins Books, 2006.

Lewis, C. S. *A Grief Observed.* New York: Bantam Books, 1961.

_____ *Mere Christianity.* New York: HarperCollins Publishers, 1952.

_____ *Perelandra.* New York: Scribner, 1944.

_____ *The Great Divorce.* New York: HarperCollins Publishers, 1946.

_____ *The Last Battle.* New York: HarperCollins Publishers, 1956.

_____ *The Screwtape Letters.* New York: HarperCollins Publishers, 1942.

_____ *The Weight of Glory.* New York: HarperCollins Publishers, 1949.

_____ *Till We Have Faces.* New York: Harcourt, Inc. 1956.

Life Application Bible. Wheaton, Ill.: Tyndale House Publishing, 1998.

MacArthur, John. *Twelve Ordinary Men.* Nashville: W. Publishing Group, 2002.

Manning, Brennan. *Abba's Child.* Colorado Springs: NavPress, 1994.

Martin, Malachi. *Hostage to the Devil.* New York: HarperOne, 1992.

Meredith, Robyn. *The Elephant and the Dragon*. New York: W.W. Norton & Company, 2007.

Möller, Lennart. *The Exodus Case*. Copenhagen: Scandinavia Publishing House, 2002.

Nietzsche, *The Gay Science*. Walter Kaufman, trans. New York: Vintage, 1974.

Oakes, Lorna and Lucia Gahlin. *Ancient Egypt*. New York: Barnes and Noble Publishing House, 2002.

Olson, Steve. *Mapping Human History*. New York: Houghton Mifflin Co., 2002.

Packer, J. I. *Knowing God*. Downers Grove, Ill.: Inter-Varsity Press, 1973.

Pascal, Blaise. *Pensée*. Trans. A. J. Krailsheimer. London: Penguin Books, 1995.

Patterson, Ben. "Uses of Enchantment." Sermon at Irvine Presbyterian Church, January 1989.

Pfeiffer, Charles F. and E. Leslie Carlson, Martin H. Scharleman (Consulting Eds). *Baker's Bible Atlas*. Grand Rapids: Baker Book House, 1991.

Polkinghorne, John. *Science and Theology*. Minneapolis: Fortress Press, 1998.

_____ *The God of Hope and the End of the World*. New Haven: Yale University Press, 2002.

Pope Benedict XVI. General Audience Address at the Vatican, August 27, 2008.

Preston, Mark. *The Monk Who Ended the Colosseum Games*. The Prayer Foundation.org.

Regele, Michael B. "Finally Faces." Sermon at Irvine Presbyterian Church, March 2006.

_____ "The Amalekite Problem." Sermon at Irvine Presbyterian Church, August 2005.

Roberts, Mark. "Finding God in Hard Times Through His Word." Sermon at Irvine Presbyterian Church, February 26, 2006.

Sahebjam, Freidoune. *The Stoning of Soraya M.* New York: Arcade Publishing, 1990.

Sanders, E. P. *Paul: A Very Short Introduction.* New York: Oxford University Press, 1991.

Scott, Darrel and Beth Nimmo with Steve Rabey. *Rachel's Tears.* Nashville: Thomas Nelson, 2002.

Simpson, George. Talk Origins.org/indexee/cg/pg110.

Slick, Matt. "Manuscript Evidence for Superior New Testament Reliability." Christian Apologetics and Research Ministry.org.

Strauss, William and Niel Howell. *The Fourth Turning.* New York: Broadway Book, 1997.

Strobel, Lee. *The Case for Christ.* Grand Rapids: Zondervan, 1998.

Swindoll, Charles R. *Paul: A Man of Grace and Grit.* Nashville: W. Publishing Group, 2002.

Tozier, A. W. *The Knowledge of the Holy.* San Francisco: Harper Collins, 1961.

Wangerin, Walter. *Paul: A Novel.* Grand Rapids: Zondervan, 2000.

Watson, Ian-Pitt. "A Kind of Loving." Sermon at Irvine Presbyterian Church, November 1990.

Watts, Rikk. "What Does It Mean To Be Human?" Sermon at Mt. Hermon, Calif., August 2004.

_____ "Why Should God Care?" Sermon at Mt. Hermon, Calif., August 2004.

Weems, Ann. *Psalms of Lament.* Louisville: Westminster John Knox Press, 1995.

White, J. E. Manchip. *Ancient Egypt, Its Culture and History*. New York: Dover Publications, 1970.

"Why Are There So Many Bibles in the World?" Hollister, Calif.: Christian Biblical Church of God. Bible Study.org.

Wright, N. T. "A New Reading of Romans." *A Royal Priesthood? The Use of the Bible Ethically and Politically*. Craig Bartholomew et al, editors. Carlisle, England: Paternoster, 2002.

_____ *Creation and Covenant*. Minneapolis: Fortress Press, 2005 @ntwrightpage.com/ wright_creation_covenant.

_____ *Evil and the Justice of God*. Downers Grove, Ill.: Inter-Varsity Press, 2006.

_____ *Jesus and the Victory of God*. Minneapolis, Minnesota: Fortress Press, 1996.

_____ "New Perspectives on Paul," a lecture. Edinburgh: Rutherford House, Dogmatics Conference, 2003.

_____ "Paul, Arabia and Elijah." *Journal of Biblical Literature*, Vol. 115, 683-693.

_____ "Paul's Gospel and Caesar's Empire," a lecture. Princeton: Center of Theological Inquiry, 2002.

_____ "Paul in Different Perspectives," a lecture at Auburn Avenue Presbyterian Church, Monroe, Louisiana, 2005.

_____ *Simply Christian*. New York: HarperCollins Publishers, 2006.

_____ *Surprised by Hope*. New York: HarperCollins Publishers, 2008.

_____ "The Paul of History and the Apostle of Faith." The Tyndale New Testament Lecture, 1978.

_____ *The Radical Jews*. Reviews in *Religion and Theology*, 1995.

_____ "The Resurrection and the Post Modern Dilemma." *Sewanee Theological Review*, 1988.

Yancey, Philip, *What's So Amazing About Grace?* Grand Rapids: Zondervan, 1997.

_____ *Prayer.* Grand Rapids: Zondervan, 2006.

Young, William Paul, *The Shack.* Newbury Park, Calif.: Windblown Media, 2007.

About the Author

 **J. Davis (Dave) Illingworth, Jr.**, was formerly Senior Vice President Chief Planning and Administrative Officer of Toyota Motor Sales, U.S.A., Inc. In this position he was responsible for Finance, Corporate Services, Business Planning, Human Resources, Information Systems, Strategic and Product Planning, Advanced Product Strategy, Telematics, Legal, University of Toyota, and Motorsports.

Illingworth joined Toyota in 1980. He held management positions in sales, customer relations, and market representation and was general manager of Denver and Cincinnati regions, as well as group vice president and general manager of the Lexus Division. He was with Lexus from the division's inception in January 1987 through 1992, and he was instrumental in making Lexus an industry leader in customer satisfaction, sales, and quality. Most recently, Illingworth was senior vice president and general manager for the Toyota Division from 1992 to 1997, overseeing sales and marketing.

In recognition of his work, Illingworth was named *Automotive News* All-Star for 1997; *Automobile Magazine's* 1992 "Man of the Year" for his leadership of the new Lexus Division; and one of the auto industry's "Top 10 Newsmakers" by *Automotive News*. One of the vehicles he oversaw, the Camry, earned the title of America's best-selling car in 1997.

A graduate of Ohio University in Athens, Illingworth earned a Bachelor of Arts degree in sociology and is a member of the Ohio University Foundation Board of Trustees. At age 65, Dave retired from Toyota and now lives in Winona Lake, Indiana, with his understanding wife, Cynthia, and is the Toyota dealer in the nearby town of Warsaw.

Dave and Cynthia have experienced the ups and downs of raising five children; Spencer, Trevor, Blair, Greer and Emily, and have learned from that experience that you are only as happy as your unhappiest child.